American Universalism

Fourth Edition

GEORGE HUNTSTON WILLIAMS

SKINNER HOUSE BOOKS (BOSTON)
UNITARIAN UNIVERSALIST HISTORICAL SOCIETY (BOSTON)

Printed in the United States

Cover design by Bruce Jones
Text design by Suzanne Morgan
Cover photo by Staff Photographer/Jane Reed, Harvard News Office

ISBN 1-55896-441-X

Library of Congress Cataloging-in-Publication Data

Williams, George Huntston, 1914–
    American Universalism : a bicentennial historical essay / by George Huntston Williams.—4th ed.
      p. cm.
    Includes bibliographical references and index.
    ISBN 1-55896-441-X (alk. paper)
    1. Universalist Church of America—History. 2. Universalism—History. I. Title.

BX 993 . W55 2002
289.1'78—dc21   2002067033

Presented at General Assembly of the Unitarian Universalist Association in Seattle, Washington, July 2, 1970.

10 9 8 7 6 5 4 3 2 / 05

Note: Throughout this book references are made to the "merger" of the American Unitarian Association and the Universalist Church of America. Though the word *merger* is occasionally used, informally, in fact the two predecessor organizations were legally consolidated rather than merged.

CONTENTS

PREFACE

The celebration in 1970 of the bicentennial of John Murray's coming to America coincided with a renewal of long-dormant interest in Universalist history. Ernest Cassara had just completed his documentary history, *Universalism in America*, and Russell Miller's encyclopedic *The Larger Hope* had been commissioned by the Universalist Historical Society. Moreover, as part of the observance itself, at the Unitarian Universalist Association General Assembly held in Seattle, Harvard historian George Huntston Williams (1914–2000) delivered an address on American Universalism. In the course of preparing that address, Williams became so intrigued by his subject, a new one for him, that he went on to expand it into a monograph, published the following year by the Universalist Historical Society as *American Universalism: A Bicentennial Historical Essay*, and republished in revised form in 1976 and 1983 as a Skinner House book.

The publication of Williams's monograph in 1971 is important for several reasons. Not only did it help foster a renewal of interest in Universalist history, but this in turn helped revitalize the Universalist component of the consolidated denomination when it appeared to be in danger of becoming lost. Furthermore, it set a high, persisting standard for Universalist historiography. After three decades, this monograph continues to be a bountiful source of information, a stimulus to further research, and an inspiration calling us to new perspectives in the study of Universalist history.

Williams was well known at the time as a historian of early Protestantism and Unitarianism, especially for his authorship of *The Radical Reformation* (1962). He taught church history at the Starr King School and the Pacific School of Religion from 1941 to 1947 and at Harvard from 1947 to 1980. He revealed a surprising Universalist heritage when he dedicated the monograph to his mother, both of whose paternal grandparents were Universalists. In the first of his many helpful footnotes, Williams also acknowledged "immense satisfaction" from the discovery, during the course of his research, of two nineteenth-century Universalist relatives previously unknown to him.

The book begins with Williams reviewing the proceedings of the centennial celebration held in Gloucester, Massachusetts, in 1870 and analyzing the state of Universalism at that time. He identifies three differing, though often overlapping, conceptions of the Universalist Church. The first is that of a sect or branch of the Christian church as a whole, initially trinitarian and Rellyan as promulgated by John Murray, but soon transformed into the unitarian, this-worldly theology of Hosea Ballou. The second conception is that of the American church of the future, closely linked to the ideals of the American republic, and the third, that of the church of universal religion grounded in the emergent world civilization. As James D. Hunt recognized in the preface to the earlier editions, Williams presents "a fresh typology of Universalist theological positions, shown in their 1870 expressions as well as in their origins and recent development . . . [and] a wholly new set of categories for comprehending the dialectics of change in the theology of Universalism."

Next Williams examines "Selected Aspects of American Universalism in Bicentennial Perspective." Included are the social reform efforts of Horace Greeley and Quillen Shinn; the ordination of women and the concern for women and children; temperance and the working class; penal reform and capital punishment; spiritualism; war, peace, and pacifism; foreign missions; relations with the Unitarians and Congregationalists; and the evolution of universal Christianity toward a universal religion. The topics are covered well and in rich detail. In his conclusion Williams properly points out that "American Universalism is a much more complex movement than American Unitarianism." Yet he maintains that throughout this movement, despite its complexity, there continues "the formative Universalist confidence that there is a powerful and benign force at work within us, about us, at the interior of being and above it, that sustains our hope."

Because the material is tightly focused, some background in theology and American Universalist history is needed for a good understanding of the book. Despite its brevity, Williams's monograph is not to be regarded as a popular introduction to American Universalism.

The publication of this present edition has been a project of the Unitarian Universalist Historical Society's republication task force, consisting of Lynn Hughes, David Johnson, Naomi King, and myself. The strong support of David Bumbaugh, Peter Hughes, and the other members of the Society's board is acknowledged with thanks, as is the enthusiastic cooperation of Patricia Frevert, publishing director of Skinner House Books, and project editor Mary Benard. Finally, we acknowledge the generosity of the New York State Convention of Universalists for providing the grant that made this republication possible.

George Huntston Williams was still alive during the initial planning for this reissue. We hoped that he would be pleased to see his work returned to circulation. When Williams passed away a year ago, Unitarian Universalism lost one of its great living historians. We dedicate this printing to his memory.

Charles A. Howe
May, 2002

This bicentennial historical essay I dedicate on the anniversary of her death 25 June to my mother, Lucy Adams Williams (1880–1969), both of whose paternal grandparents were Universalists, Philo and Lucy (Adams, Upham) Pease of Chardon, Ohio. It was an immense satisfaction to the author in preparing this essay to have located the names of a collateral relation, Amos Upham of Newbury, and presumably an ancestor who was a physician, "Dr. [Pelatiah] Adams" of Hambden and Chardon, in the MS Minutes of the Western Reserve Association, Ohio, 1832–1853; UHL, Ohio No. 19, pp. 2, 5, 8, 21, 22, 46.

GHW
1971

INTRODUCTION

One hundred years ago, for three days in an unusually dry September in Massachusetts, the Universalists of America celebrated in Gloucester the preceding century of their movement in what the metropolitan papers freely acknowledged was the largest organized religious assembly to date in the history of the country, with 12,000 present at the peak.[1]

Although John Murray (1741–1815) had landed on American shores in 1770 at Good Luck in New Jersey, it was entirely appropriate to commemorate a century of organized Universalism in the town in Massachusetts where Murray had his first settled pastorate. It was appropriate in any case that the centennial celebration take place in New England, where various currents had converged to make of it the most Universalist part of the country.

To be sure, there were early onsets and tendencies elsewhere in America toward Universalism as the gospel of God's benign intention to save all men (perhaps all creatures), for example, in the Middle Colonies as symbolized by the expectancy of Thomas Potter of Good Luck, Murray's winsome host. But as a denomination Universalism was generated in New England.

The quite distinctive German and Moravian Pietistic universalism (with its English Behmenist and Philadelphian counterparts)[2] entered what was to become the main body of organized anti-

Calvinist denominational Universalism by way of the proclamations and publications of Massachusetts-born Baptist Elhanan Winchester (1751–1797), who for seven years was a universalist evangelist in the London meetinghouse of the Philadelphian Society (1787–1794), where he converted William Vidler (d. 1816), his successor there.

Complex, even disparate perhaps in its origins and in its successive affluents, American Universalism was, nevertheless, broadly speaking, preeminently an anti-Puritan upthrust in New England, and it spread *denominationally* to the middle states and to the south only after the amalgam of the Murray and the Winchester ingredients had been pretty well melted and mixed in the crucible of New England fireside and cracker-barrel discussion, conference debate, and tractarian controversy. Denominational Universalism was the rural and small-town counterpart of seaboard Arminianism/ Unitarianism in renouncing the somber Calvinist views of man and God in New England and later in those other regions of the emergent Republic where Calvinism in its Presbyterian or Orthodox Congregationalist and especially Baptist forms was the dominant version of Christianity. The first annual General Convention of Universalists outside the Puritan-Presbyterian-Reformed region of New England and New York was in Philadelphia in 1837.[3]

The common witticism found no formal expression at the Centennial, to wit, that rural and small-town Universalists in their reaction from Calvinism "believed that God was too good to damn them" for all eternity, while in contrast the seaboard-urban Unitarians, prospering under free enterprise, held that men like themselves "were too good to be damned."[4] But the principal Unitarian at the Gloucester Centennial, Edward Everett Hale, in his official greeting in another idiom and metaphor, implied an awareness of this distinction. Combining the Univeralist stress on the love of God and the Unitarian stress on the loveability of men, Hale declared in 1870, "If America is to fail, it is because the doctrines of Calvinism and the Roman Catholic Church are true; if America is to succeed, it is because God is love, and loves each and all of his children."[5] One reason that Hale, like other speakers at the Centennial, was prompted to bring in Catholicism alongside Calvinism was that the affirmation of the dogma of papal infallibility at the I Vatican Council[6] and the fall of Emperor Napoleon III[7] were in the minds of centennialists thanks to the but recently laid transatlantic cable.[8] But if the global and the domestic threat of authoritarian Catholicism was very much to the fore as a consequence of the heavy Continental immigration to the cities of the North that followed the end of hostilities with the slave-based autocracy of the South, the fact remains that both Unitarianism and Universalism were essentially anti-Calvinist rather than anti-Catholic in their New England genesis.

Nor can Hale conceal from us, even though in the euphoria of the Centennial he may have veiled it from his loudly applauding and jovially laughing Universalist audience, the sociocultural fact that his striking indisposition to consider denominational federation between the two liberal churches was grounded in an instinctive aversion on both sides to mingling two denominations of markedly different regional and class origins. Said he, as official spokesman of the National Conference of Unitarian and other Christian Churches,

> I have no wish, in coming here, to suggest, even by an innuendo, any consolidation or any fusion of the bodies here represented. If it were my duty to carry from Boston to the great Pacific anything which I considered was of infinite value [namely, Christian liberalism], I should not take it in a wheelbarrow. I should be sure to find some wagon [an allusion to the but recently completed Union Pacific[9]] which could run upon a broad track . . . if I would go successfully to my journey's end.[10]

To move from the one wheel of a wheelbarrow to the two tracks of a train was not orator Hale at his metaphorical best, and, although he was not, of course, likening Universalism to the rural wheelbarrow and Unitarianism to the interurban and transcontinental train, still the rural–urban contrast between the two liberal Christian denominations will surely have gone through his mind as he prepared his remarks, coming out by train from Boston to Gloucester. But then there was something besides the class and regional differentiation between Universalists and Unitarians to which he was rightly alert, otherwise he would never have introduced his wheelbarrow–train paragraph with so strong a word as "innuendo." And this other consideration was his awareness that many Universalists, in Centennial Convention assembled, were themselves strongly opposed to any link with the Unitarians[11]; and this opposition was based, among other things, on quite distinctive views of the universal and comprehensive mission of organized Universalism on its own.

We can do no better a hundred years after the Gloucester Centennial than to try to understand what it was in Gloucester that made Universalists so confident in their continental and global mission and that Hale himself sensed in not presuming at that time to suggest any kind of Unitarian–Universalist merger.

The speeches and lesser communications at Gloucester in 1870 were full of a uniquely Universalist theme. To be sure, Universalists had met to do honor to John Murray as the founder of American Universalism in the city where he was ordained. (His first visit there was in 1773; the church was organized in 1779. He was minister in Boston, 1793–1809.) They were in the process of completing their centennial denominational endowment in his name, the John Murray Centenary Fund (of $200,000). Somebody from Vermont had brought Murray's faded cloak, but no one knew exactly what would be appropriate to do with it.[12] A lady speaker brought a moving message and reminiscence from an elderly woman doctor whom Murray had baptized in childhood, but the orator had not quite found the time to fetch the Bible once inscribed by Murray and offered by the invalid doctor as a precious memento of the patriarch to be exhibited at the Centennial.[13] And many of the celebrants were in possession of the Centennial Edition of *The Life of Rev. John Murray* written by himself with a continuation by his second wife, Judith Sargent Murray,[14] for which Thomas Whittemore had supplied notes for editions since 1833 and which was supplied with more notes, an introduction, and illustrations by Dr. Gerherdus L. Demarest for the Centennial edition (1870).[15] But even the editor acknowledged, referring to Murray's "peculiar opinions," "It is probable that no living man or woman now entertains them in their wholeness."[16]

To be sure, the effort was made to bring over from Watertown the communion silver that Murray had once imported from England, and this was duly employed for the solemnly joyful communion service in the tent.[17] To be sure, also, the whole company made a pilgrimage to Murray's original meetinghouse, two miles out from Gloucester and now converted into a barn, but decorated with wild-flowers for the occasion by the Orthodox Congregationalist farmers.[18] But surely, the overwhelming impression of all things said at the Centennial is that the peculiarly Christocentric humanitarian "Calvinist" Universalism of John Murray of Alton, England, and of Good Luck, New Jersey, had been largely transcended and trans-muted in the variant new theories of salvation and the ecclesiologies, articulated or euphorically presupposed in most of the addresses in Gloucester. Murray's cloak was scarcely less faded and outworn than his particular version of salvation and his particular ecclesiology.

In brief, Murray under the influence of James Relly, within the theological framework common to both Calvinism and its softer version, Arminianism, postulated Jesus Christ, fully human and fully divine, as the Second Adam, who literally took upon himself man-kind as a garment,[19] one with his nature, so that his expiatory act of utter obedience to God the Father redeemed all mankind, past, con-temporary, and prospective—"the common salvation" (Jude 3). Murray, when clearest, distinguished between universal redemption and the knowledge thereof, which is salvation from guilt and anxi-ety. For him, the purpose of preaching the gospel was to inform his auditors of the good news of what was already a fact, namely, their having been redeemed. For Murray the church of the redeemed was, therefore, theoretically coterminous with humanity, past, present, and future; but in a narrower sense the church was that portion of mankind, i.e., that portion more specifically of Christendom, who had become gradually aware of the revolutionary implications of the gospel.[20] Murray called this Universalism "the Gospel preached unto Abraham" and the response thereto "Abrahamic faith." His mystical conception of Christ's headship of the race or recapitula-tion of mankind as the Second Adam would survive in muted and quite altered form as the distinctively Universalist component of the denomination's latter-day global humanism.

Let us hear again what they were saying at Gloucester in the first chapter, scrutinizing the not entirely congruent conceptions of what the Universalist Church was, then in the second chapter examine some representative personalities, episodes, issues, and themes during the hundred years after that celebration and two hundred years after Murray's arrival. By centering on the denomination in 1870, we can perhaps with selective detail, in fairly brief compass, acquire a bicentennial perspective on the essential character of Universalism and tentatively assess the impact of the Universalist Church in America and its ongoing contribution to the larger body of which it is now a part.

UNIVERSALIST CONCEPTIONS
OF THE CHURCH, CIRCA 1870

In the General Convention of Gloucester in 1870, Universalism completed the overhaul of its ecclesiastical structure, as did many another denomination after the Civil War, adopting a comprehensive new constitution for "a uniform organization of the Universalist Church."[1]

To understand Universalist ecclesiology, at least as well as Unitarian Edward Everett Hale presumably sensed it, will help us assess the impact of Universalism on American society at large; for the doctrine of the church is, as it were, the social or sociological component in every theology.[2] As the Universalists at Gloucester thought expressly of the church, so also thought they indirectly of society emerging from civil war and of Western civilization suddenly restructured by the emergence on the world scene of four imperial nations: the II Reich of Bismarck of 1870/1871[3]; the Kingdom of Italy fully unified in 1870[4]; the Russian Empire freed of serfdom since 1861; and the United States reunited and freed of slavery in 1865. At the same time Catholic Christendom, through the dogma of papal infallibility enunciated in 1870, was experiencing a spiritual sublimation of the Roman imperial impulses in both dogmatic authoritarianism and redoubled inter-international political action through concordats and Catholic parties. Universalists, now much more at home in the big cities and mill towns than in their forma-

1

tive period, were in 1870 keenly conscious of the Universal Church of Rome, represented in their midst by the rapidly growing parishes of immigrants of alien speech or manner, while one of their own distinguished preachers, Orestes A. Brownson (1803–1876), had in 1845 actually converted to Catholic universalism.

What were some of the Universalist conceptions of the Christian church in general and their church in particular at this momentous juncture in world history?

Theoretically and indeed constitutionally, the General Convention of Gloucester in 1870 represented the high point of denominational unity in the expression of its faith, for it incorporated the Winchester (New Hampshire) Declaration of Faith in three brief articles (1803) and required assent thereto[5]; and, to give substance to this consolidation of denominational mood, provisions were made for a board of appeals to be appointed by the board of trustees of the General Convention to hear cases of doctrinal and professional misbehavior of ministers in the state conventions that might appropriately come before it. Yet, even in the Gloucester proceedings and discourses, given the limited scope of the Declaration of 1803, the range of conceptions of the church was considerable, for that Declaration had had nothing to say expressly on the doctrine of the church, only about the final restoration of "the whole family of mankind to holiness and happiness."

Before we listen to the individual expressions in 1870, let us try to have before us tentative patterns of reference. There were, it would appear, about three main views of the church with a few variants of each. All variants in the warm and expansive mood of Gloucester could have been accepted by almost everyone present, but to distinguish them conceptually is to identify certain deep impulses in Universalism as of 1870, which would be clearer in the hundred years to follow. Broadly speaking, two of these components would lead to the merger with Unitarians in 1961. One of them would account for the perennial combination of cordiality and reserve, pique, and even rancor with respect to the Unitarians in the nineteenth century, leading at times a large contingent and even temporary majorities toward the efforts first at union with the Congregationalists in the early 1920s and then at membership in the Federal Council of Churches of Christ in the 1940s. Since this third component view is closer to the original impulse of Universalism two centuries ago, though now largely superseded, we shall characterize it first.

We shall call the first conception of the church somewhat arbitrarily *Christian universalism.* Its most visible marks after the Centennial were a heresy trial in 1872 and the dispatch of a converting, baptizing mission to Japan in 1890. Speaking bicentennially, Christian Universalism has manifested itself in three successively overlapping phases or variants of emphasis in the Universalist interpretation of itself in the Christian economy. Two of these phases were rehearsed and celebrated in the Centennial Sermon delivered by the Reverend Dr. Alonzo Ames Miner, president of Tufts College.

About these two phases, we are today perhaps clearer than Dr. Miner could be in his day. In the first phase of Christian Universalism, two quite disparate and disproportionate universalist impulses had been struggling within the fellowship for clarification. John Murray, in his sermons of 1770 and thereafter, had cast his thought in the much enlarged framework of Calvinism and had proclaimed the Rellyan good news of redemption in Christ in union with all mankind. Murray had scriptural sanctions for his Universalism (John 12:47; Rom. 5:6; I Cor. 15:22; Col. 1:20; I Tim. 2:4; Jude 3). Elhanan Winchester, with the mysticism and millennialism of Georg Klein-Nikolai, the Reverend Sir James Stonehouse, and Dr. George de Benneville (in the place of James Relly for Murray), without perhaps knowing it was more in the line of Origenism, holding to an eventual restoration of all creatures, not, however, without varying degrees of eschatological purgation. In a word, the Universalism of Winchester, drawing on Pietistic, Moravian, and Philadelphian eschatology, *looked forward* to an eschatological restoration of all creatures, not, however, without some painful purgation *in the afterlife* for the sinful, whereas the Universalism of Murray, drawing upon the distinctive Christology of Relly, *looked back* to the definitive and decisive recapitulation of the human race by Christ as the Second Adam and affirmed that mankind was already saved for eternity and had but to be apprised of this in preaching and seized of this faith to enjoy this redemptive security already *in this present life.*

3

The double orientation of American Universalism in the first phase to the redemptive past and the redemptive future constituted the central dynamic of this remarkable American body of come-outer Christians. At the same time, in this first phase, the universalism of both leaders, the Massachusetts-born London evangelist and the English-born Boston pastor and denominational father, was still functionally and expressly trinitarian.[6]

Phase two of Christian Universalism was a unitarianizing Universalism under the impact of *A Treatise on the Atonement* (1805) by Hosea Ballou, 1st (1771–1852), and of the *Ancient History of Universalism* (1829) by Hosea Ballou, 2d (1796–1861), of Tufts, who stressed the preeminence of free will among the Greek fathers and dwelt on such patristic analogues and antecedents to Winchester and Murray's proclamation as Origen of Alexandria. This annexation of this primitive Christian and patristic heritage, for a while dominant in the denomination, was preeminently the accomplishment of President Miner's predecessor at Tufts. Phase two was thus a fully Unitarian Universalism with the stress no longer on the afterlife, but simply on the constancy of the divine benevolence in all stages of creation and on an uncalculating human benevolence in response to the divine plenitude of purpose. Universalists in this mood were joyfully energized to accomplish much in serene indifference to the whole system of rewards and punishments of most Protestants in their environment (and of Catholics, where they encountered them).

Evangelical Protestantism had changed considerably since Martin Luther's first proclamation of salvation by faith alone over against medieval works—righteousness embedded in a moral theology of merits of congruity and condignity for salvation. Indeed a system of means, merits, and signs of salvation had been so massively, even though precariously, built up in nineteenth-century Protestantism that in a quite valid sense we can identify in the Universalist nonchalance about the afterlife amid the sometimes morbid anxiety and moralism of surrounding revivalistic and evangelical Protestantism the very spring of Universalist moral energy comparable to the role of Luther's uncalculating and exuberant *sola fide* salvation in the first Protestant generations.

With Murray, Winchester, and the two Ballous, Universalists were confident that redemption (Murray) or atonement (Ballou) had already been achieved for all mankind, and it remained only to free (save) those still seated in the anxious darkness of the Calvinistic scheme of election, reprobation, and the bondage of the will: to save them in the sense of helping to "reconcile" them to the "simple scriptural fact" that they had already been saved! This is what Ballou implied in the subtitle of his *Atonement:* "Its Glorious Consequences in the Final Reconciliation of *All Men* to Holiness and Happiness."[7]

To an extent, all the participants in the Gloucester Centennial were still caught up in this second phase of Christian Universalism, which, however, would not long endure in the same intensity. For their serene confidence in universal immortality (whether with or without some purificatory chastisement) was initially based upon Christ's divine–human headship of, and mystical union with, mankind and the consequent universal efficacy of this atonement; but the gradual shrinkage of the Adamic and eschatological Christ of Murray and Winchester into the Nazarene teacher of parables of most of the Gloucester spokesmen required a gradual reconception of Universalism and of the church embodying the new thrusts.

An ensuing third phase or variant of Christian Universalism, namely, a moralistic Unitarian, Jesus-centered universalized Christianity, was already well articulated by Thomas Baldwin Thayer in his *Theology of Universalism* (1862). The first comprehensive systematic theology in the denomination, often reprinted, it was almost wholly scriptural without reference to the ancient or American fathers of Universalism. We shall find this the prevailing version of Christian Universalism after 1870.

The second main conception of the church and salvation articulated at Gloucester, no less Christian, to be sure, in intention than the preceding, was that of *Republican Universalism,* that is, of Universalism as the church of America, as the "Democracy of Christianity," as that form of Christianity most congruous with the professed ideals of the Republic, now once and for all freed to express itself continentally and indeed around the world by reason of the removal of the hideous blemish of slavery in the body politic through the surgery of civil war. To be sure, at its inception, American Universalism, like primitive Christianity, was in its sectarian mood respectful of the powers ordained by God, distant from them and at the same time alert to any overwhelming claims of government, whether royal or republican. The Articles of Association of the original Universalist Church in Gloucester in 1779 had declared:

> [W]e will be peaceable and obedient subjects to the powers that are ordained of God, in all civil cases; but as subjects of that King whose kingdom is not of this world, we cannot acknowledge the right of any human authority to make laws for the regulating of our conscience in any spiritual matters.[8]

Some four score years later, Universalists in a churchly mood felt themselves to be much more a responsible part of the establishment. Thus, in a sometimes spread-eagle mood, more than passing satisfaction could be taken by War Governor Washburn of Maine, for example, a major architect of the Centennial, in George Washington's having commissioned John Murray as a chaplain in the Revolution despite opposition from the mainline Protestants. The main difference between Republican Universalism and comparable affirmations in other denominations, including the Unitarian,[9] is that the Universalists claimed that theology, and polity, and above all theodicy made of them the most distinctive bearers of the ethos of the Republic. It was not hard for all Americans in the wake of the Revolution and then of the Civil War to think of themselves, like Revolutionary France (and later Revolutionary Russia) as the vanguard, spokesmen, and representative embodiment of humanity.

The third conception of the church and salvation among some Universalists in 1870, though not expressly articulated at Gloucester, might seem scarcely distinguishable from the first and indeed quite assimilable to the second. But it was different. It was the view that Universalism represented both the primitive form of Christianity and the future form of world religion. Whereas the Origenistic–Arminian and evangelical forms of Christian Universalism considered as the democratic Christian counterpart of the American Republic stressed the present and the immediate future development of post–Civil War American society, *Restitutionist World Religion Universalism*, to give it a label, was at once communitarian,

6

vaguely millennialist, and eventually world-religionist in its tendency. It was restitutionist in the sense that it sought to restore primitive Christian norms. This could also be called a restorationist thrust, as with the Campbellite Disciples of roughly the same period, but for the fact that the term is preempted with a specialized meaning by the Universalist schism of the Restorationists, 1831–1841.[10] Moreover, since the universalism of the primitive church was but a specialized version of the original Abrahamic faith, spoken of by Murray, restitutionist world religion Universalism could also look forward to the universalization of their faith as the world religion. This hope was transfused, of course, with the same Transcendentalism that brought about a kindred mood in Unitarianism. The ecclesiological thrust of this third kind of Universalism would keep the Universalist Church from any uncritical identification with American democracy and would finally lead to a distinction of Universalism from Christianity as "the Religion for Greatness,"[11] preserving in its global humanism, however, only faint traces of Murray's formative conception of Christ as mystically the head of all mankind. Although this concept was not widely shared in 1870, it was pregnant with the future, while still drawing nutriment from the Winchester tradition and the German sectarian millennialist-purgative ingredient he had introduced.

There were three foci of this partly pacifistic, working-class–oriented impulse in the nineteenth century: (1) the futuristically oriented communitarianism of Adin Ballou, as he outgrew a Universalist Restorationist phase and which, though not articulated at Gloucester, was formulated at Hopedale in lectures given in the same year, 1870; (2) the Catholicizing solution of communitarian Universalism in idiosyncratic Orestes A. Brownson (ordained Universalist, 1826; envisaged the "Church of the Future" in connection with his Society for Christian Union and Progress, 1836; converted to Catholicism, 1844; died 1876);[12] and (3) the conviction that Universalism was the highest and most comprehensive form of Christianity, which, under the influence of evolutionism, Hegelian idealism and its German-American antecedent, transcendentalism, would first be given expression in the sermon on natural religion by Herman Bisbee in Minneapolis in March 1870 (leading to a heresy hearing and suspension in 1872). Much later this component in Universalism would lead to the organization of the Community Church in Boston in 1920 and to the fellowship of the Humiliati at Tufts with their off-center cross in the larger circle of world religion in 1945.

We turn now to the particulars of three conceptions of Universalism as expounded in 1870.

CHRISTIAN UNIVERSALISM

Origenistic-Arminian-Unitarian Universalism

Surely the most characteristic view at Gloucester in 1870 was that of the Convention Sermon, a comprehensive survey of Universalism from Christian Antiquity to the Centennial by the Reverend Dr. Alonzo Ames Miner, at the time President of Tufts (1862–1874). President Miner took as his texts Rev. 22:13 "I am the Alpha and the Omega" and II Peter 3:8 "One day is with the Lord as a thousand years"[13] and proceeded to rehearse the history of Universalism in the context of a broad appreciation of philosophy and natural science.

A gathering in Boston of Unitarians in this year would never have thought it expedient to listen to so long an address on the history of Unitarianism. Indeed it was only in 1850 that a historian of British Unitarianism, first organized in conventicles in the mid-seventeenth century, began annexing Polish Socinianism and Transylvanian Unitarianism as part of the pedigree[14]; and when, a century later, Earl Morse Wilbur would come in America to publish the definitive history of the Unitarian movement,[15] he was obviously ill at ease in trying to go behind the Reformation Era to antiquity and to include Arius of Alexandria among the roster of forerunners. But Miner in 1870 still felt very much at home with Clement of Alexandria and Origen and he was addressing a throng all of whose older members had been instructed by the Universalist histories of Hosea Ballou, 2d and Thomas Whittemore to think of the Christians of the first centuries as Universalists.[16] Miner, following his mentors, was quite willing to include any number of mystical Gnostics among the forerunners of the Universalist faith, in the Middle Ages the Cathars, and in the Reformation Era the Anabaptists. He was also keenly sensible of the fact that in contrast to English Unitarians, their American counterparts were initially indisposed, from their lofty establishmentarian status in society, to countenance universal salvation;[17] and that Charles Chauncy of First Church, Boston, despite his *Salvation for All Men Illustrated and Vindicated as a Scripture Doctrine* (1782) heartily disliked John Murray and all his emotional works. Miner was fully aware that Universalism in America had "Begun, like Christianity [in antiquity], in the lower walks of life"[18] and no doubt saw therein historic sanction for, and promise of, an imminent rise of Universalism to prevalence in America.

Dr. Miner readily acknowledged his indebtedness for his quite moving sweep of Universalism through nineteen centuries to the historical scholarship of his presidential predecessor Hosea Ballou, 2d (1796–1861)[19] who, as a young preacher, after working in Harvard College Library with the encouragement of its President Josiah Quincy, had published his *Ancient History of Universalism* (1829). Ballou's work had carried the history of Universalism from the apostles to the Gentiles down to the V Ecumenical Council in 553, which condemned Origen and all his works, including Universalism. An appendix carried the account more sketchily through the Reformation Era. Then Thomas Whittemore (1800–1861)[20] had published the continuation of that account as *Modern History of Universalism* (1830), with the last three chapters on American Universalism. The two related works were presently to be followed by the two volumes of Richard Eddy, *Universalism in America* (1884/86).[21] These four volumes represent together an important theological and historiographical achievement in a distinctively Universalist stress on scripture and on history in contrast to American Unitarianism, which at its inception, as already noted, made no comparable attempt to reclaim a lost or invisible history and annex an ancient heritage.[22] Unitarians, instead, exerted themselves rather to make plausible their claim to being the logical continuators of the Puritans and Pilgrims not only in the ancestral first parish meetinghouses but also in their covenants and congregational polity; they did not contend that benign John Cotton or philanthropic John Chrysostom were essentially Unitarian! No more significant contrast, therefore, can be drawn between American Unitarianism and American Universalism than the confident essay of the latter to write itself into universal Christian history. This Universalist sense of history with a millennial goal ahead is the clearest testimony to the group consciousness of their being something new. Like Continental Baptists (Anabaptists) in the sixteenth century and English Baptists in the seventeenth century, American Universalists cultivated historiography in contrast, for example, not only to Unitarians but also to Lutherans and Calvinists in the sixteenth century (both of whom had professed to be the authentic continuators of pure apostolic and patristic catholicity) and in contrast to Methodists in the eighteenth century, who likewise were very slow to produce a distinctively Methodist interpretation of even Anglican history to say nothing of general church history.

Thus the Centennial Sermon of President Miner was a characteristically Universalist attempt to claim sanction and authentication from proponents of universal salvation and the limited punishment of sin in the afterlife wherever this testimony could be shown to have cropped out and almost regardless of the doctrinal company it might have appeared with. President Miner, going beyond historians Ballou and Whittemore, assimilated into the general system of Universalism (understood as the gospel of the divine progenitor constant in love, chastening his children but not in vindictive and endless punishment) the evolutionary, utilitarian, positivistic views of Theodore Jouffroy (d. 1842),[23] John Stuart Mill (d. 1873), Charles Darwin (d. 1882),[24] and Herbert Spencer (d. 1903). But for all his valiant updating, the ministerial president of Tufts may be allowed to stand as the only official spokesman at the Centennial Convention of the older trinitarian Arminian-Origenistic and subsequent Unitarian conceptions of the Universalist Church in the line of the founding fathers Elhanan Winchester, John Murray, Hosea Ballou (1771–1852),[25] Hosea Ballou, 2d, and Thomas Whittemore.

Universalism: A Christian Sect or Branch of the Church of Christ?

The Reverend George W. Skinner of Quincy, Massachusetts, called attention during the Centennial to the fact that by the recent organization of the General Convention, Universalism was "now a church and no longer a loose denominational organization."[26] Skinner had a few years before indeed identified "Universalists as a Christian Sect,"[27] and had gladly appropriated James Freeman Clarke's characterization of the denomination as "The Democracy of Christianity," remarking, "Probably since the reformation under Luther, no one movement has accomplished so much for others, while achieving so much for itself."[28]

The conception of the Universalist Church as a sect or branch of the Universal Church of Christ, in modification of the conception of the church in the founding fathers of the denomination, was given ample expression at the Centennial, among others by the Reverend Dr. Richmond Fisk, president of St. Lawrence University (1868–1872), by the Reverend W. H. Ryder of Chicago, by Dr. Edwin Hubbell Chapin of New York City, and by Dr. Elbridge Gerry Brooks of Philadelphia. These four men, while they considered Universalism "a distinctive branch of the church," did not therefore regard other churches as mere deformations of true Christianity, as was the case of many in the first two generations.

President Fisk restated Murray's salvific doctrine without reference, however, to his predestinarian context, but still confident in a distinctively Universalist mission among the denominations, "[W]e are educators of the Christian church universal upon this one point—that you can have all that is essential in the teachings and the life of Jesus Christ, and carry on his church, independent of the fear of hell or the hope of heaven as the chief incentive."[29] With Fisk it was no longer the paternal benignity of God that precluded endless punishment, but it was rather the morality and rationality of man that made the doctrine of rewards and punishment ethically unnecessary as the motivation of good conduct:

> [W]e stand before the world as a Christian church, utterly bereft of and having cast away all the old hopes of heaven for having done our duty, and all the old fears of hell if we do not do our duty.[30]

Dr. William Henry Ryder of Chicago cast the same thought in more practical denominational terms:

The great need of the Christian world is a knowledge of Universalism, but the great need of the Universalist denomination is quite another thing. . . . There are a number of men all over the country who believe theoretically in Universalism, and I am thankful for that; but that does not build up the Christian Church very much, and it does not build up our denomination. . . . I want the doctrine that universal salvation implies universal obedience preached; that every man is born into the kingdom of our Lord through faith in Jesus Christ, and becomes a consistent Universalist only when he consecrates his life to the good of his church and to the welfare of this world.[31]

Ryder here and throughout his address gave evidence that his denomination (which had once proclaimed universal salvation amid theological sneers) was now faltering because the collapse everywhere of the invisible predestinarian superstructure had left it without an engine to promote participation in churchly activity ("mutual obedience," as he called it).

By far the most eloquent spokesman of Christian Universalism at the Centennial was Dr. Edwin Hubbell Chapin (1814–1880).[32] Sometime pastor of Universalist churches in Richmond, Virginia, Charlestown, Massachusetts, and in Boston a colleague of Hosea Ballou (1st) at the School Street Church, he had been since 1848 pastor of the Fourth Society in New York (the Church of the Divine Paternity). Dr. Chapin in the long communion sermon heard by 7,000 in the tent on Thursday afternoon declared, "There is a deeper church than the Universalist church, it is Christ's church; and remember that outside of all churches and creeds, there are thousands and hundreds of thousands, who have no fixed, definite views, who do not know exactly what they believe. They know one thing—that they believe in Christ."[33] Celebrants who were familiar with the writings of John Murray or had refreshed their memories with a reading of the Centennial edition of the autobiography, will have heard this as a muted echo of Murray's formative conversion conviction that Christ saves the unbelievers as well as believers.[34] Chapin had already made explicit in his communion meditation, "We cannot say this is a Universalist, a Unitarian, a Presbyterian, or a Baptist table. *This is the Lord's table!* We dare not seal it with our creed."[35]

A publisher of sermons and discourses in several popular volumes, Dr. Chapin would formally state his understanding of the church in "The Church of the Living God," later to be preached on Whitsunday as the commencement sermon before the graduating seminarians at Tufts in 1878.[36] Drawing upon the Göttingen church historian Johann C. I. Gieseler[37] and others rather than upon Ballou and Whittemore, Dr. Chapin would argue for a comprehensive ecclesiology: "[The Living Church] is limited to no sect, but comprehends the entire mass of Christian believers. It is characterized by no exclusive ceremonial. . . . It holds a wide diversity of intellectual views."[38] He goes on in this spiritualizing pan-Christian vein, "This church comprehends all that is true in the past, all that is right in the present, all that is good in the future. Unity is the antithesis of monotony—it is the consummation of divinity."[39]

Dr. Chapin's understanding of Universalism within the Christian tradition was thus irenic and broad. Let us return to his Centennial sermon. Thinking of "the wide banyan tree of Christianity, that stretches from land to land, and from shore to shore,"[40] he deplored the sad fact that the "rite, which should have been the Feast of Love, and the bond of union for all Christians," had often been the occasion of strife. He rehearsed at Gloucester the historic formulations (from simple commemoration to transubstantiation) to affirm his conviction that in the uniquely "divine life in Jesus" as "our Saviour," Universalists could join with all Christians in recognizing in Christ the universal mind, transcending that of any race or culture to interpret the whole of life and to give healing and direction to the "abandoned, the deluded men who are plunged deep in the world's cares, the world's pleasures, the world's business, the world's perplexities."[41] With a glance at the calm September Atlantic, he declared

I hold that Christ alone interprets life; the mystery of life; the dark, sad passages that stream in here and there. Mysteries, my friends, that come down upon life as before long the cold and dark tempest will come sweeping down upon yonder beautiful sea. It will be tossed in wild commotion, and that which lies today sleeping, as it were, with an infant's sleep, shall be a wild, irresistible force, driving strong men and even navies to destruction. So ever and anon there breaks in upon life those incidents which . . . have their interpretation only through the life which is Jesus Christ. [42]

Certain that "it is a better work to make men Christians than to make men Universalists,"[43] Dr. Chapin was nevertheless confident that to Universalists was "committed the power of salvation and redemption," with special reference to "the churchless and the skeptics," to "the low slums of humanity, for the poor waifs and castaways, the harlot, the unclean, the shamed and despised,"[44] because the Universalist Church stressed the lordship of Christ without reference to future rewards and punishments. Near the close of the communion sermon, addressing perhaps more the unregenerate without than the seven thousand within the tent, Dr. Chapin spoke the language of a rational evangelical revivalist, "God lives for you; Christ died for you. Battered coin of God Almighty, there is something of the Divine image and superscription there yet! Bandaged, swathed about with sevenfold cerements of sin, God's love shall work in your heart until you shall strip them from brow and lips, and stumble, like Lazarus, into a new and regenerated life."[45]

Dr. Chapin had thus preeminently an evangelical spiritualizing sense of the church. He would acknowledge that the gospel might indeed find notable expression in the Universalist denomination, but he considered the church as inclusive alike of the hearts of hundreds of thousands of would-be followers of Christ outside organized religion as well as of believers in the highly organized denominations of Christianity.

Perhaps the most distinctively Universalist version of Christian Universalism was that of Dr. Elbridge Gerry Brooks (1816–1878) of Philadelphia. His might almost be called High Church Universalism in that he had a clearly articulated view of the Universalist Church as something grand with the promise of the future, transcending and then leading Roman Catholicism, evangelical Protestantism, and the world to the universal Christ. Born in Dover, New Hampshire, named after Vice President Elbridge Gerry, he studied law before theology, the latter privately in Portsmouth under the ministerial father of Thomas Starr King, and he was successively minister in Cambridge, New York, and Philadelphia.[46]

Dr. Brooks was the main force behind the creation of the General Convention, serving it also as the general secretary from 1868 to 1869,[47] and the theorist of the polity of the Universalist Church as shaped by the Centennial Convention, whereby the Universalist Church emerged as far more integrated and disciplined than the loose congeries of autonomous congregations of the original New England setting where Universalists had been recruited so strongly from among Baptists. Chairman of the committee on revision of the Constitution of the Universalist Church,[48] whose report was accepted with little alteration to become the basis of the church in 1870,[49] he afterwards set forth the rationale for this in "The Church" in *Our New Departure: or, The Methods and Work of the Universalist Church of America as It Enters on Its Second Century* (ch. xiv).[50]

Brooks was strong in his view that the local church, centered in the Lord's Supper, should be distinguished from the parish (the term "society" was eschewed), made up of both communicant members and associates who together sustained the temporal aspect of the meetinghouse. This ecclesiological distinction was written into the Constitution adopted at the Centennial.[51] Above the local church and parish were the associations, state conventions, and the General Convention to constitute the Universalist Church. The state and general conventions, strengthened by the Centennial deliberations and decisions, had had to wrest some power from the venerable regional associations of face-to-face fellowship, which in the West particularly were virtually churches in their own right controlled by the laity, often without clerical franchise.

Brooks, in his more theoretical retrospective presentations, distinguished four meanings of the word "church:" (1) humanity, "the body of which Christ is the head," e.g., with reference to Ephesians 5:25 and in perpetuation of a theme of Relly and Murray;[52] (2) "the whole organized family of Christian faith," that is, the whole Christian community or visible Church; (3) the local company of the faithful; and (4) the Church invisible and visible, that is, "the vast company of the redeemed on earth and in heaven."[53] Actually, a denomination like the Universalist Church constituted a fifth meaning, as a branch of item 2, Christendom, and elsewhere, indeed, Brooks would specifically call Universalism "a living branch of *the* One Church."[54] But for Brooks, the Universalist Church, in its new departure from the euphoria and impetus of consolidation at Gloucester, was far more than just one more American denomination. It was nothing less than "the Church of the Future."[55] It was the church of the future because, if true to its commission, it would supersede Roman Catholicism and evangelical Protestantism (by moving in effect from item 4 above to item 1).

To effect this end, however, Universalists, building on the Constitution perfected at Gloucester, would have to get away from the idea of the great mass of "Protestantdom" that the church "is a mere voluntary association,"[56] "educating the people to feel themselves foreigners to the Church . . . , to feel that the Church is nothing to them."[57] Nor should the church be thought of as "a kind of religious pound," into which people are driven for safe keeping until death.[58] From Catholicism Universalists must with other Protestants learn that the church is something given, "an ordinance of God," like the state and the family, "a trinity of primary institutions,"[59] and that of the three the church was founded expressly by Christ. As much as he admired Roman Catholicism for its liturgy and art[60] and to an extent also for its imposing ceremonies[61]; for its capacity to nurture saintly lives[62]; for being "one of the most wonderful organizations for effective religious work . . . [which] we can, and should, copy,"[63] he also feared the Catholic Church for its holding its members in "vassalage to Church rule,"[64] its neglect of civil liberty[65] and education for the masses, and its fostering of "beggary, ignorance, general shiftlessness."[66]

Likening Universalism to David, Brooks set forth his great hope:

> The rising David cannot be clothed in the armor of the doomed Saul. [He was thinking of the High Church liturgical revival in Episcopalianism.] The Church of the Future is to be a vitalized Protestant Church, and not a rejuvenated Roman Catholic Church with the Pope left out. David must wear his own armor, and do his better work in his better way. But excluding all that is inconsistent either with our ideas of motive or with our notions of liberty and the right of private judgment, and speaking only of what is unobjectionable to

us in Catholicism as to the spirit and practical sagacity of its methods, as to Church ideas and underlying principles, as to winning, formative, holding powers, these, as Catholicism has combined and availed itself of them, are essential and permanent [for us, also] . . . .[67]

With a change of reference we get the whole of Brooks' concept:

[O]ne of the purposes of the Universalist Church, in the Providence of God, . . . is so to interpret what the Church is, and so to press what it demands as, in this failure of "evangelical" Protestantism [with its neglect of the Church and Christian nurture in the stress on revivals], to supply what the time in this respect requires. Universalism harmonizes reason and faith, and is thus able to present an ideal of the Church equally satisfying to both. It alone gives us the Church *republicanized*.[68]

Brooks had to acknowledge that in large measure Universalism had undergone "some of the worst influences" of fissiparous evangelical Congregationalism and individualism, but he was somehow confident that Universalism as now emerging could help the world understand "the Church as the perpetual symbol of religious ideas and as the means of communicating spiritual life,"[69] for the "outward Church is the body and symbol of the spiritual family of which Christ is head, and of which all united to him in faith and love are members."[70] He went on: "[T]he Church is the natural and organic relation of souls born into the kingdom of God through the ministry of His Son; . . . the channel through which God communicates His Holy Spirit and saving power most directly and potently for the enlightenment and redemption of souls."[71] Because of its redeeming power Brooks felt that the church, besides its two sacraments of baptism and communion, should "help towards the Christian life through the closer and more sympathetic relations with which it binds its members" by means of "vows," including "mutual watchfulness."[72] It is clear that the chief architect and contractor for the Universalist Church of America as of 1865, 1870, and 1871 was a High Churchman. It would be this component in Universalism that would so long account for its very fervent sense of a massive mission in American Christianity, over against which Unitarianism might seem to some Universalists but an austere sect. The American destiny of

Universalism as the superior form of Christianity, as also the most fitting religion for the future Republic, which we find in the Brookses, ministerial father and novelist son, has already brought us well into our next major Universalist conception of the church.

UNIVERSALISM:
THE AMERICAN CHURCH OF THE FUTURE AND THE CIVILIZED WORLD

The Centennial Convention was exposed to a second distinguishable theory of the Universalist Church, neither the branch theory of Ryder, Fisk, Skinner, and Chapin nor the attenuated Arminian-Origenism of Miner. It was closer to the Christian Church of the Future of Brooks, except that it had much more audible Americanist overtones. This second, humanitarian, quasi-millennialist Americanist theory was expressed at the Convention, among others, by Israel Washburn and Mrs. Mary Livermore. It may have found sanction in the Winchester Profession of 1803 in the first two articles in reference to the "final destination of *mankind*" and in the confidence that the one God of love "will finally restore the whole family of *mankind* to holiness and happiness"; but the immediate context of this renewed conviction was the salvation and purification of the American Republic itself in the recent Civil War and was, for some, emotionally linked with the doctrine of American manifest destiny. Although the intentions of all who held this view were no doubt global and humanitarian, the instrument of their universal hopes was American democracy sustained by Universalist–Christian nationalism. A religion of American democracy was implicit in much that was stressed in this view of the Church in 1870 and thereafter. It goes back in Universalist history as far as Elhanan Winchester's tricentennial *Oration on the Discovery of America* (1792) and his poem on *The Process of Empire . . . to the end of the mediatorial kingdom,* published posthumously (1805). Universalists in a nationalist mood in 1870 were perhaps overcompensating for having long suffered from such orthodox baiters of Unitarians and Universalists as the Reverend Ezra Stiles Ely (1786–1861) of the Christian Party and author of *The Duty of Christian Freemen to Elect*

Christian Rulers (1828). Ely, like President Timothy Dwight (d. 1819) of Yale, feared for the nation because of the Universalist want of fear of eternal punishment in the afterlife. Attempts to keep Universalists out of public office, off juries, and generally out of public life energized their fight to participate fully in the democratic process.[73]

Israel Washburn (1813–1883), antislavery lawyer, a founder of the Republican Party, war governor of Maine, was a trustee of Tufts College. He began this Centennial address a little bit like Brooks, by saying, that "Strictly speaking, the Universalist is not a Protestant Church."[74] He went on to distinguish between the Church of "God's love unlimited," his own, and the Church of "God's love limited," by which definition the "Catholic and Protestant churches are substantially the same." The earlier terminology here had contrasted the two as the Universalist and the Partialist Churches.[75] But Governor Washburn no longer presupposed the double-predestinarian background of this older terminology. Moreover, though he began, as Miner (or Ballou or Whittemore before him) might have done by assuming that these two groupings were to be found from the beginning in the church, he was soon in a mood to proclaim that the Universalist Church "would upheave and displace a [limited love] church that upon the fundamental ideas of Christianity was unsound."[76] Holding that the Universalist Church based on God's unlimited love was "more than Catholic as that term has come to be understood," he professed that it was "universal in its scope and ultimate membership—it will embrace the world." He put Protestants and Catholics on the defensive, holding them to be "but a temporary instrumentality and not the final church"[77]; and he urged Universalists to be steadfast "for the upbuilding of the Church which shall best represent it [God's unlimited love], until that Church shall become the church of Christendom and Christendom shall be coextensive with the earth."[78]

Thus in contrast to President Miner and to President Fisk, Governor Washburn, in having effaced the whole system of two eternal decrees presupposed by the formative Puritanism of New England and in stressing only the abiding benignity and redemptive purposefulness of God, was completely freed from the theological past, both from the aboriginal divine mind (as understood by St. Paul, St. Augustine, and John Calvin) and from the primitive church, to stress almost wholly the future of the church of God's impartial love, destined to become coextensive with humanity. Moreover, Governor Washburn linked this prospect with American manifest destiny.

Not only did Washburn think of Universalism as the vehicle of the Church Universal, but he also thought of the American nation as its political counterpart. In the same address he noted the providential coincidence of the Boston Massacre of 1770 and the landing of John Murray at Good Luck to preach Universalism in New Jersey. "In that *annus mirabilis*," said he, the emergent Universalist Church of America and the impending democratic Revolution made their appearance providentially together. He went on: "It was the faith of John Murray upon which alone could be maintained the declaration 'that all men are created equal; that they are endowed by their Creator with certain unalienable rights.' " "It is obvious that these fundamental principles of this government are identical with those of Universalism, and are radically inconsistent with those of the old Church."[79] Following the speech the band quite appropriately, though scarcely at Governor Washburn's express request, played "Hail Columbia." The same feeling that the Universalist Church and the American Republic were in league had already been expressed by a committee, made up of Washburn among others, commissioned to plan for the Centennial now unfolding. The year before at Buffalo they had said,

> The new century . . . is to witness an advance of the Nation . . . a result never before possible to American civilization, because cursed with the barbarism of slavery. It will also witness, as its religious characteristic, the supremacy of that church whose doctrines give the most unmistakable support to its advanced civilization. All harsh and *partial* theologies will surely be outgrown and repudiated . . . *The American Church of the future,* based on the divinity of Christ and his God and the brotherhood of man . . . must . . . rely, for its organized effort, on those who are already faithful to these Christian doctrines. Universalists of America! For you the closing century has prepared this glorious privilege of the future![80]

This same feeling for the Universalist Church of America would be notably expressed also just three years later by one in attendance at the Centennial (celebrating a centennial of his own local church in Portsmouth, New Hampshire), "Our church has a right to be called the Church of America. The genius of our Religion is perfectly at one with the genius of our Government." Alluding to George Washington's having made Murray a Revolutionary War chaplain "against the protestations of half the sectarian chaplains,"[81] the celebrant at Portsmouth insisted in line with Washburn at Gloucester, "The history of our church and our Government run parallel from the beginning."[82] Arguing like Washburn, he said, "You cannot supplant a *false* Church with no church at all"; and he exhorted "the ablest men" of the other denominations to "come out and join our church" to augment it fourfold and *"cripple* every other church in America, while we would become an army that no man could number."[83]

To return to Gloucester, after the band interlude, Governor Washburn was followed by Mrs. Mary A. Livermore (wife of the Reverend D. P. Livermore) of Melrose, Massachusetts. During the Civil War Mrs. Livermore (1821–1905), who for three years had taught school on a Virginia plantation, raised relief funds and organized nursing facilities under the Sanitary Commission. Later she would become president of the Massachusetts Women's Temperance Union, an officer of the Women's Educational and Industrial Union, the Women's Congress, and a trustee of a medical school. She long labored for women's suffrage, and she preached in different pulpits about half the Sundays of the year. At Gloucester she spoke on two recorded occasions. She implied much the same view of the Universalist Church as Governor Washburn, expressed, however, in unusually ardent and appealing feminist tones.[84] She made bold to say, up to John Murray's proclamation of Universalism, that "the Church of the past had not been a Christian church, but pseudo-Christian."[85] To be sure, this was a perfervid exaggeration of the moment, for she had given another speech the Wednesday evening before[86] in which she had with learning and conviction shown how women had been powerfully creative in the antifeminist and slave culture of the Greco-Roman world and had sustained and later had enlarged the faith within the bosom of medieval and even modern Catholicism, citing indeed two Roman Catholic instances of her point.[87] But basically her conviction and her orientation was like that of Washburn toward the future of Church and society, and she had said in her Wednesday speech before women only, "Universalism is . . . synonymous with Christianity."[88] Her look was eschatologically to the future rather than restitutionally to the past: "Through the doctrines of Universalism, I expect sin to be overcome." "[W]e mean more by the doctrine of God's fatherhood than do the other denominations." "Christianity [of which Universalism is the most consequent expression] is to conquer this world; to kill out its sin; to win it to God; to swing it forward to that blessed time that prophets have foretold and poets have sung, which we call 'the golden age,' 'the good time coming,' 'the millennium'; and if you prove to me that I am a fanatic, a visionary, an enthusiast on this point, then you prove to me that Christ has lived and died in vain. . . . And that I will not believe, for Christianity is of God, an outcome of his nature, and He is immutable and omnipotent."[89]

In her Thursday speech, following Washburn, she still more excitedly repeated the same confident turn of argument, but with even greater afflatus as she addressed a plenary session and not the ladies alone. Alluding to Washburn's address, she too affirmed her own conviction that in Murray and the Massacre that led to the Revolution "the Lord God had been making ready for the introduction of Universalism"[90] and of a new nation responsive to God's omnipotent love manifest now alike in the September collapse of the Catholic Empire of Napoleon III and but five years before in the final expurgation of slavery from the American Republic. She went on: "I tell you that we are today pressing on with hot, swift feet to the great, grand time . . . to which the hearts and minds of the whole world reach forward, and we shall have but one worship, that of the Universal Father, who embraces in His nature every form of love known to us, loving creatures of His; when we shall recognize the great tie of brotherhood the world over; when we shall be done with wars and battles; when we shall come together as one people, with the Lord God our Father and our Leader."[91] Mrs. Livermore, having seen as a young teacher the inhumanity of slavery on a relatively humane Virginia plantation, wished that she had been able herself to fight for the Union cause like a man.[92]

We turn now from the closely related views of Mrs. Livermore and Governor Washburn[93] in their hope for the unity of mankind through something between a Universalist America and American Universalism as the instrument of God "by which the world is to be won" to the third main conception of the church among Universalists, c.1870.

UNIVERSALISM:

THE WORLD RELIGION OF THE GRECO-ROMAN WORLD

AND THE EMERGENT WORLD CIVILIZATION

As of 1870 we can record two and, in their time, quite measurably distinct variants of the conviction about Universalism as the World Religion: the natural religion of Herman Bisbee and the "millennialist" communitarianism of Adin Ballou. Neither of these views was expressed in Gloucester, although they had something in common, respectively, with Washburn's Universalist Church, neither Catholic nor Protestant, and with Brooks' "Church of the Future."

The Reverend Herman Bisbee (1833–1879), minister of the Universalist Church in St. Anthony, Minnesota, delivered in March 1870 a sermon entitled "Natural Religion" in Minneapolis across the river, wherein he opposed the Rev. J. H. Tuttle's position on miracles and on the sufficiency of Scripture.[94] (Tuttle was a delegate from Minnesota at Gloucester and would be a major factor in bringing down upon Bisbee the charge of heresy.) Said Bisbee in the opera house of Minneapolis, in the manner of New England transcendentalists and spokesmen elsewhere of the Free Religious Association:

> I believe that Jesus taught Natural Religion, and claimed to teach nothing more. . . . There is no creed from his lips; no ceremony imposed. . . . [H]e would not persecute; he would not ask us all to believe alike; he would say: "Be true to conscience; seek, trust the Father and fear not. . . ." In Natural Religion there is no gift. Salvation does not come by grace. All the priests in the world cannot pray a soul out of its natural purgatory. . . . Jesus taught goodness, and this is Natural Religion. It is my opinion that a man can believe one thing or another, and still be a Christian, but when a man becomes mean, he can no longer be a Christian.[95]

This vigorous expression of transcendentalism in a Universalist minister was exceptional. It along with a subsequent series of "Minneapolis Radical Lectures" led to Bisbee's suspension from the Universalist ministry in the Minnesota Convention, confirmed by the General Convention in 1872. But we may pass over it as an unrepresentative episode in 1870 to attend to a much more significant, though also isolated figure, Adin Ballou.

Though Adin Ballou, in 1870 a Universalist minister of a Unitarian parish, enunciated views that were perhaps uniquely his; nevertheless he caught up into his thought the whole of Christian Universalism of the Origenistic–Arminian cycle and must be presented as a symbolically important figure, even though he was not present at Gloucester nor, as far as can be determined, even referred to. It must be acknowledged that his communitarian Universalism, being very close to the Origenistic–Arminian type of the founding fathers of the denomination but largely superseded by the more generalized Christian Universalism of a large proportion of the Gloucester celebrants, would seem improperly bracketed with the transcendentalist natural religion of Bisbee, but Adin Ballou, like Bisbee, stressed so much the future unitive religion of the world that in a sense he saw the "Universalism" of the primitive Church in the Greco-Roman Empire repeating its miraculous success in the fullness of time in becoming the humanitarian religion of the impending world civilization. Moreover, as a pacifist of sectarian mentality, he could not go along with either Universalism as the church of America as it was or with the Christian Universalism of a denominational type that had largely lost its eschatological and even millennialist fervor. And what he described as the religion of the Roman Empire conquering evil by love and peace was an abstraction of historic Christianity that could appear to successors in this line as the religion for greatness with such faint Christian traces that it could be regarded by the time of Dean Clarence Skinner as equivalent to world religion, to the natural religion of Bisbee, as just characterized. It was to be a recurrent phenomenon in Universalism in its second century that it would frequently assert either the identity of a highly generalized Universalist Christianity as the world religion or, breaking through Christianity, assert that Universalism as the world religion must relegate historic Christianity to an off-center position (see pages 64–78).

Adin Ballou (1803–1890), the most articulate exponent of Restorationist Universalism as embodied in trinitarian John Murray and notably Elhanan Winchester, had joined in 1831 with seven other ministers to form the Massachusetts Association of Universal Restorationists.

The schism was something of an anomaly in being unrepresentatively named and localized.[96] Universalists differed as to the duration and divine purpose of limited chastisement in the afterlife (over against eternal punishment in ambient orthodox Protestantism). Winchester had believed in limited future atonement—but limited to 50,000 years! Ballou in his *Atonement* (1805) taught that chastisement was limited to the earthly life and would never concede punishment in the afterlife unless it be for sin committed after death. A principal in the debate ensuing, Charles Hudson, characterized Ballou's position in refuting it, *The Doctrine of Immediate Happiness of All Men at the Article of Death* (1823). Eventually defenders of some kind of chastisement in the afterlife would go on to characterize the view of Ballou and associates as "Death and Glory Universalism." The schism of 1831–1841 in part received the name Restorationist because one of the principals on that side (Jacob Wood) had signed himself "Restorationist" in the increasingly acrimonious debate that led to the schism in Massachusetts. It is noteworthy that not even the majority of those in Massachusetts who held to a limited future punishment went out in the schism and that elsewhere the two positions (Death and Glory vs. Probation) persisted side by side. Adin Ballou said that Unitarians favored the Restorationists and he surmised in 1871 that by then nine-tenths of the denomination were holding to the views of the former schismatics, namely, to limited chastisement for the achievement of holiness in the afterlife.[97]

After the schism, in 1841, Adin Ballon established the Hopedale community, which in turn had dissolved in 1868, when it merged with the Hopedale Parish (Unitarian).[98] It was as minister of this church that Adin delivered a series of lectures, the first volume of which was printed precisely in the year of the Centennial as *Primi-*

tive Christianity and its Corruptions (1870). Despite Adin Ballou's absence from Gloucester, a survey of Universalist conceptions of the church a hundred years ago would be incomplete without a characterization of his distinctive view.

The entire third volume of Adin Ballou's in part posthumous book is devoted to his conception of the church. The first volume had dealt with theology, the second with personal righteousness, and the third with what he subtitled "ecclesiastical polity."[99] Under this heading he dealt with Christ as intentionally founding a church and he proceeded to characterize the essentials of the true Christian church, supplying reasons for its early defection from the divine human community as established by Christ. He thereupon discussed in nine chapters the principal Christian groupings, as he felt it appropriate to deal with them: the Roman Catholic and Greek Orthodox Churches together, then the Church of England, down through Moravians with Friends, Christian Disciples with Swedenborgians and Shakers, to a final lecture, in which he characterized American Universalism and Unitarianism *ca.* 1870, finding them both wanting! It is with this concluding chapter that we pause for his insights and characterizations.

Adin Ballou distinguished three classes of people who became identified with Universalism a century earlier: (1) "a few profoundly and truly religious persons—benevolent, conscientious, devout," to whom the idea of eternal reprobation was emotionally unendurable because of their understanding of God as benevolent; (2) a "larger class" to whom the idea of reprobation and endless punishment was intellectually absurd and rationally indefensible; and (3) "such persons as usually hang upon the skirts of any new movement that seems to promise them immunity from irksome restrictions, larger liberty of thought and conduct, and more personal ease, comfort, and enjoyment."[100] At the time of the lecture, he saw the first class of the sensitive devout increasing; the second, the rationalists, improving; and the third slowly and happily vanishing.

He acknowledged the origin of Universalism among humble and largely uneducated people.[101] He was confident, however, that their insight and "distinguishing characteristic, . . . a belief in the doctrine of the final holiness and happiness of the whole family of mankind," had slowly permeated "the more conservative and tradition-ary churches, until at length it gained the respect of all fairminded people, and, to a considerable extent has modified, if it does not dominate [*c.* 1870], the belief of the church universal; showing that the day of its triumph is dawning and will ere long burst in glory upon the world."[102] But if the Universalist *doctrine* had proven so influential and promising, what had Adin Ballou against the Universalist *Church* of his time?

He found the Universalist Church unsatisfactory because, despite its doctrine, it too palpably conformed to society and nation. After criticizing the Winchester Profession of Faith (1803) as insufficiently specific, he went on to his basic criticism of the Universalist Church in 1870, of which he had so long been a minister, on much the same principle that informed his sustained critique of all denominations as inadequate or even deceptive:

> [The Universalist Church] does not propose or set up any higher or more Christlike standard of personal, domestic, social, or civic virtue or excellence than that which is represented in so-called civilization, whose potency and final appeal center in statute law, in vindictive punishment, and in the supremacy of injurious force and violence in the last resort. It vies with the Calvinistic, Arminian, and other classes of professing Christians, in subordinating Christianity to worldly governmentalism in its practical application to human affairs. It seeks to build up no kingdom of God on earth distinct from and superior to the existing social and political order. So that were all men converted to Universalism, *as it now is,* the world would go on very much as it now does. . . . I therefore look for a truer, higher, more Christlike one [Church], yet to be established on the earth.[103]

It is clear why Adin Ballou was not at Gloucester!

Ballou at Hopedale was not only a pacifist, but he also refused to discharge any civic duties (see further below, "Selected Aspects of American Universalism in Bicentennial Perspective" in the section "War, Peace, and Conscience"), so profound was his sectarian-eschatological sense of the disparateness of the true church and the world. His was a very special form of Restoration, the restoration of the primitive church of Jesus and his apostles before corruptions had set in. Regarding the true church as a fellowship reflecting the ideals of the imminent kingdom of Christ, he regarded it also as itself an instrument in that impending universal event. Accordingly, he distinguished within and about the fellowship "orderly members, dependents [progeny], and attached probationers," self-subsistent "without slavish and humiliating dependence on . . . the outside world,"[104] and for the maintenance of "the unity and harmony of all Christlike souls," he required "just reproof and disfellowship of evil-doers."[105]

His critique of historic and Boston Unitarianism was like that of Gloucester Universalism—irenic, clear, and loftily devastating:

> I conclude that the Unitarian Church with all its excellencies is not the church of the New Dispensation—the church that is to inaugurate the divine kingdom on the earth. . . . I find [it] . . . wanting in some fundamental elements and requisites of a true church of Christ according to the primitive pattern. I remand it, therefore, with others I have examined, to a subordinate place in the providential economy of the world and in the work of establishing on the earth the long deferred reign of truth, love, righteousness, brotherhood, peace, and joy.[106]

Adin Ballou, himself a lonely Universalist minister of the local Unitarian Hopedale parish, after his Hopedale community had dissolved, could still declare in sublime imperturbability, "I confidently expect and prophesy the rise at a not very distant day of a new and regenerate form of the Christian church; one occupying a much higher plane and conforming much more closely to the primitive ideal than that which now exists."[107] He concluded his chapter on the twin denominations, that is, his third volume on the Church, and in effect the whole tripartite work on primitive Christianity yet to be restored with the following poem:

> Almighty Maker of the countless spheres,
> Father of Christ and all the holy seers,
> How long must prayerful faith expectant wait
> Thy promised kingdom in this mortal state?
> When, through the true, the Christ-like Church renewed,

The race of man with love shall be imbued;—
When all on earth shall know and do thy will
As all in heaven thy perfect law fulfill.[108]

SELECTED ASPECTS OF AMERICAN UNIVERSALISM
IN BICENTENNIAL PERSPECTIVE

The three interrelated concepts of the church represented in 1870 were to survive *mutatis mutandis* up to the merger with the Unitarians in 1961.

The third, that of Adin Ballou, embodying an authentic and indeed important impulse from the early days of the movement, was already a museum piece when being outlined in lectures at Hopedale; but that component in the denomination at large would merge with the transcendentalist natural religion of Bisbee and other less conspicuous spiritual kinsmen to aliment in the twentieth century the Universalist humanism most characteristically embodied in Clarence Skinner's Community Church of Boston.

The view of Governor Washburn, among others, that Universalism represented the most authentically American version of Christianity would live on to inform the political conduct and denominational rhetoric but it would inevitably be dissipated in the general tendency of various Christian denominations or groupings in the religiously neutral constitutional Republic to propose themselves as sanctions and custodians, on the right, of Christian America, and on the social gospel and humanist left, of American civil liberty. A clarification of the Universalist role in the widespread conviction as to America the Redeemer Nation needs, however, much further detailed study.

The development and permutations of the conception of Christian Universalism are easier to follow, as it is the component that resisted merger with the Unitarians and sought, rather, to take on for the denomination the attributes of a plenary Christian body. The view of Dr. Edwin Hubbell Chapin and others in 1870 that Universalism is essential Christianity and is but one of its many denominational manifestations would in due course find expression in a Universalist mission abroad on the model of that of other denominations and live on as the impulse that would lead to a later attempt to join the Congregationalists (1925–1927) and twice to join the Federal Council of Churches (1944 and 1946) and to resist the merger with the Unitarians, but it, too, contained within itself the seed of world religion (see below, as for example at n. 21, this chapter, and pages 75–78).

TWO REPRESENTATIVE EXPONENTS OF THE CONCERN OF UNIVERSALISTS WITH THE REFORM OF SOCIETY[1]

Universalists were, by 1870, prominently associated with women's rights, the integration of the freedmen into American society, fair labor arrangements, temperance, nonsectarian education, the humane treatment of children and animals, and political reform. Two attendants at the Gloucester Convention may be taken as symbols and embodiments of many of those aspirations: one approaching the end of his career, Horace Greeley (1811–1872); the other at the very threshold of his career, Quillen Hamilton Shinn (1845–1907); one, the denomination's most prominent layman; the other, its chief animator and home missionary. Horace Greeley may be taken as the lay embodiment of Universalism after the period of Father Hosea Ballou (1771–1852) when Universalism was felt to be the unofficial but veritable Religion of the Republic, that is, the democratic, republican, idealistic, and prophetic version of Christianity for the New World (as much in the religious as in the geographical sense of that phrase). In contrast, Quillen Shinn, the ordained youth worker and planter of new, mostly white, Universalist churches and institutions in the South, embodies the more denominational conception of

Universalism that prevailed from the Centennial to the opening of the First World War.

Horace Greeley of the New York State delegation at Gloucester was founder and reform-zealous editor of the *New York Tribune* (1841). He was a parishoner of Dr. E. H. Chapin at the Church of the Divine Paternity. He took an expansive and jovial part in the contested seating of the Maryland delegation, all from one congregation (!), and read the report on "Diffusion of Universalism,"[2] in which it was urged that the Murray Fund be used to print and distribute 100,000 volumes on Universalism and at least a million tracts annually. The report would indicate that Greeley was familiar with a number of standard Universalist books, but of his religion we read little in the numerous biographies.

In his own autobiography,[3] published just the year before the Centennial, Greeley in a chapter "My Faith," concentrated on an episode in ancient Greek history that had struck him when a lad of about ten in his birthplace, Amherst, New Hampshire. It was the mercy that the conqueror Demetrius Poliorcetes showed toward the prostrate Athenians, who had earlier treated him less generously. And Greeley concluded, "Reflecting with admiration on this exhibition of a magnanimity too rare in human annals, I was moved to inquire if a spirit so nobly, so wisely, transcending the mean and savage impulse which man too often disguises as justice, when it is in essence revenge, might not be reverently termed Divine [which] . . . must image and body forth that of the 'King immortal, invisible, the only wise God' [I. Tim. 1:17]."[4]

By way of a printing press, young Greeley became acquainted with Universalism, understood as the preachment of the divine benevolence and magnanimity, but it was not until he came to New York City from Erie, Pennsylvania, that he formally joined a Universalist Church, that of the youthful Rev. Thomas J. Sawyer, of which he remained a member until Sawyer left, whereupon he joined that of Dr. Chapin. An earlier letter to an editor fills in our knowledge of the scope and depth of his Universalism.[5] Believing "that an Omniscient Beneficence presides over and directs the entire course of human affairs, leading ever onward and upward to universal purity and bliss," Greeley knew that he differed from the original American Universalists in that he rejected the doctrine of the Trinity, but like them he believed that due chastisement would continue in the afterlife and that "the very wicked here will never be quite so well off as though they had been good." He went on, "I judge that Mary Magdelene is now, and ever will be, in a lower grade than Mary the mother of Jesus."[6] Greeley had also been open to the claims of vegetarianism, Fourierism, and communitarianism—more that of Fanny Wright of Neshoba, Tennessee, or of Robert Owen in New Harmony, Indiana, or of George Ripley at Brook Farm in Roxbury, Massachusetts, than that of somber Adin Ballou in Hopedale. It was in allusion to the latter, however, that Greeley could write that his religious views had "generally accorded nearly with those held by the Unitarian Restorationists,"[7] combining thus in this unexpected phrase the two New England influences in, and parallels to, his personal faith.

Horace Greeley, as he stood before fellow delegates in Gloucester, was known to all as an opponent of the Mexican War and as a Free Soiler; as an outspoken opponent of slavery, who in his signed editorial "Prayer of Twenty Millions" of August 1862 had assailed President Lincoln for not having made emancipation Federal policy instead of compromising with the sensibilities of the border states; as an equally vigorous champion of reconciliation with the defeated Southerners and an opponent of wage slavery in the Northern industrial towns; as a champion of labor unions and cooperatives; as a defender of women's rights (save on the issue of suffrage); and as a (destined to be unsuccessful) candidate for the House of Representatives in the November elections of that very year. Two years hence Greeley would be the candidate for presidency in a coalition of the Liberal Republicans in convention in Cincinnati and of the Democrats against President Grant in pursuit of a second term and would proclaim that South and North were now "eager to clasp hands across the bloody chasm." Carrying, to the surprise of everybody, only six border and Southern states, he was disheartened and died insane that very autumn. The divine magnanimity, however, that he had so much admired in the Grecian general Demetrius came to expression in General Ulysses S. Grant, who with his vice-president, the chief justice of the Supreme Court, the governors of New York and

New Jersey, and countless other notables was in attendance at the immense funeral presided over by Greeley's minister Dr. Chapin, assisted by Henry Ward Beecher and Dr. Thomas Armitage.

Quillen H. Shinn (1845–1907),[8] who was graduated from St. Lawrence in 1870 and who saw the ocean for the first time when attending the Centennial from his first parish in Vermont, may be taken as a representative denominational figure in the expanding horizons of domestic mission and reform in the period after the Civil War up to the Declaration of Social Principles in the General Convention of Worcester, Massachusetts, in 1917.[9] Born in Virginia, Shinn fought as a youth with the newly formed West Virginia Union forces and wrote home to his mother, after the first battle of Manassas or Bull Run:

> it is offel to see the entrenchments made by the seceshenists. there is twenty-three or fore rebel graves in fifty yards of our camp. my this is a pleasant place here ... the union cause ganed the day out at manassas. they killed 25, Thousand rebels and got about 12. Thousand killed, there is plenty good peaches here.[10]

After being further educated at St. Lawrence, Shinn would write and speak with less exaggeration and a good deal more compassion, especially for the former "seceshenists."

After his pastorate in Vermont and other appointments, he eventually became national missionary for the Young People's Christian Union (beginning in 1893); and from 1895 until his death in 1907 he was the official of the General Convention charged with domestic missions. He organized summer conferences for thousands to "generate missionary power" at the (Methodist conference center) Weirs on Lake Winnepesaukee, 1882–1898. These were moved to Saratoga and then in 1901 to Ferry Beach, Maine, discovered and beloved by Shinn. "If we ever had a St. Paul in the Universalist Church it was Quillen H. Shinn."[11]

As "the wandering nomad of Universalism," a missionary primarily in the sense of denominational extension (especially in the South and West)[12] and a general animator of denominational action in convention, commission, and conference, Shinn for years ran a special column in the *Leader*, "Report from the Mission." Perhaps the most moving formulation of his mature convictions is his "Affirmation of Universalism" in the characteristically entitled *Good Tidings,* which he compiled in 1900.[13]

He accepted as his authorities "the book of nature, the book of human nature, and the book of revelation," "convinced that these three books agree."[14] Reading the book of nature in line with John Murray with a sustained sense of its beauty and purposiveness, filled also with emblems of deep meaning, thankful "for the thronging delights in this lower mansion of our Father's House,"[15] he was confident that neither a single atom nor a single soul could "get beyond the reach of this Almighty force of love so that it is unable to draw it back" and could affirm:

> We believe no such catastrophe [as eternal discord] can happen. Nature means victory. Therefore we read Universalism from this book. Every law operative here, and all the laws relating our world to other worlds, are prophetic of victory. Nowhere in this universe do we read a prophecy of defeat. [16]

Shinn's reading of the book of human nature likewise led him to renewed confidence, in this case, in the divine image in every person, and also to the realization that even "those who have made greatest progress are still in the Father's primary school." As for chastisement and salvation, as Shinn construed the texts of Holy Writ, he formulated his three points about God's Almighty love: (1) that it never changes, (2) that it never lets go, and (3) that it punishes to cure; and his six points about divine punishment: (1) that it is a spiritual medicine, (2) that it is intended to cure, (3) that it is absolutely necessary for a moral universe and a just and loving Father, (4) that it lasts until it has accomplished its purpose, (5) whether now or in the afterlife, (6) wherever the guilty soul is.[17] He understood this process of salvation to be a turning from "everlasting" to "eternal" existence, "To be saved is not going somewhere after one becomes righteous; it is *becoming* righteous."[18] He was confident that Christ would succeed in curing all men of sin because "He has medicine enough," "sufficient skill," and "sufficient time to administer the medicine in" as "the good physician." How different this view of Christ and God and their plan for the human race, he exclaimed, from that of the various orthodox Christians, "Universalism affirms a perfect God . . . Calvinism limits his goodness. . . . Arminianism limits his power."[19] Parrying the common opinion that the Universalist Church "is founded upon negations," Shinn insisted that its "affirmations express stronger faith than that professed by any other church on earth."[20] Indeed, Universalism "includes all that is good and true in all religions ancient and modern, in all systems, in all philosophies, in all churches, in all worlds, and in all the universe." He goes on:

> I accept the Christian religion as the infallible, the authoritative religion, because it takes up into itself and embodies all that is good and true; excludes only that which is false. There are but few Christians today who will not agree with us in the universality of the Christian religion in respect to its provisions. . . . *We* affirm that it will be universal in its *results*. And until all Christians shall come to believe that the religion of Christ will be universal in its results, the denominational name . . . must be retained. . . . Only in this sense, therefore, are we under obligation to remain sectarian. Loyalty to truth demands it of us. . . . I say we believe more than any other Christians. We do if the whole is greater than a part. We stand for the *whole*. Our system of faith must include all truth that has been discovered, and all that is yet to be discovered. Hence it is a progressive faith. [21]

Shinn's peroration was a sustained sentence of almost two pages, much too long to quote, of beautiful images and phrases drawn from a lifetime's perusal of the three books of nature, human nature, and scriptural revelation.[22]

Having briefly characterized two representative Universalist figures, both of whom were at Gloucester in 1870—one, whose career closed in 1872, the other whose career closed in 1907—we shall now take up some of the specific concerns that animated these two men and their fellow Universalists in their age.

As we intend to stress the second century of Universalism, looking back from the Centennial only to pick up themes that persisted or, in permutations, continued to give shape and power to the ongoing denomination, we shall first link each topic with what was said or done at Gloucester or was elsewhere articulated by Universalists around 1870 and then look backward and forward from this vantage point.[23]

Perhaps the most conspicuous feature of the Centennial Convention for outsiders was the prominence of women in the Universalist
cause. In any event, we shall take up the concern for women and
children as our first topic. It is of interest that the cause of abolition
and then that of the freedmen were originally closely united with
the cause of women's rights. It should be said, moreover, at the out-
set of this treatment that Universalism at once enhanced the feminine role and concurrently the paternal role in the Universalist
household and also in the Universalist vision of church and society
at large. To put it lapidarily, there was in Universalism more of conflict between woman and husband/father than in other denominations. On the one hand there were liberationist forces at work in
Universalism that swiftly enhanced the status of woman leading early,
for example, to her ordination to the ministry. On the other hand,
the stress on the divine paternity and benignity undoubtedly worked
also to shape the self-image and the denominational image of the
minister (characteristically laureated as a benign D.D., well before
fifty) and to shape the image also of every Universalist husband and
father. A study of Universalist domestic life as reflected in numerous
family journals and columns and church school curricula and
children's columns would be instructive, as also a special study of
the father image[24] in John Murray's extraordinary autobiography,
which must have enjoyed a paradigmatic role over the years of its
frequent reprintings. But for the nonce we concentrate on the re-
lease of female energies in the denomination and its contribution to
the feminist causes of the century.

Accounts of the Centennial drew attention to "the number of
earnest and efficient female members" among the Universalists.[25]
Besides the already-cited Mrs. Livermore, who preached much from
the pulpit but was not ordained, the Reverend Augusta J. Chapin
(1836–1905) of Iowa addressed the Convention, setting forth her
conviction that in Christ there is neither male nor female.[26] In 1893
she would be made an honorary doctor of divinity by Lombard
College, the first woman to achieve that honor in America.[27] Further

research is needed to explain the prominence of women in Universalism and their entry into the ministry.

The author of *Our Woman Workers*[28] offered a plausible explanation when in her spirited preface she accounted for the eclipse of the theological stress in the divine benevolence and of the esteem for women and children in the New Testament and the early Church as the work of "the most unhuman of men—Augustine—a man of gigantic intellect and influence, which were exerted in behalf of darkness and error."[29] Having frequented brothels in his youth and then discarded his concubine, leaving his son without legal parents, Augustine built his whole theological life "in direct hostility to that sacred relation, the paternal, on which Christianity is built. . . . He buried the Father out of sight beneath the Lawgiver and Executioner. . . . He invented Calvinism before Calvin, and his statement of Christianity was literally man-made; for the head, the heart, the hand of woman never assisted the fierce masculine artifices." After arguing that a woman theologian could never have seen in "Every cradle . . . a nest in which a moral viper was cherished," the author queried rhetorically:

> Who can doubt that the monstrous deformity that so long usurped the place of genuine Christianity would have been an unborn horror had the wife, and mother of Augustine cooperated with him in the interpretation of the teachings of Jesus? . . . . Calvinism, Arminianism, Partialism in any form is in the worst sense of the words a masculine faith, destitute of all feminine grace. . . .[30]

The author went on to give the married Reformers due credit for the restoration of true Christianity and observed that even with the advent of the Universalist Church men were by far in the majority. "But as the glad tidings spread apace it was discovered that the new-born faith was more essential to the highest needs of woman than to those of man."[31]

Mary Livermore had said almost exactly this at the Centennial. When she had spoken of "every form of love," she had in mind not only her experience of ministerial companionship with her husband, but also her experience of maternal love, which, in a compelling sentence, she related to the special religious aptitude of women commonly superior to that of men:

[T]he experience of women is deeper and more peculiar than that of men, for they go down into the valley of the shadow of death, and win the child of love by struggling for it with death itself, and then this dearly-bought child is part and parcel of their own nature.[32]

Because of this law of maternal nature, which is more like that of God the Father than that of paternal nature, women without surcease or without any value judgment except that of love ever sustain the helpless, restore the discouraged, heal the hurt, find the lost and the bewildered, subdue the proud. Accordingly, she said, "Christianity signifies more to women than men, and especially to the women of my church, who have this large interpretation of Christianity given them."[33] Mrs. Livermore recognized that a woman had been a factor in the conversion of John Murray and that the second Mrs. Murray, a "strong-minded woman," had given "a good and generous backing."[34]

The first denominationally ordained woman minister[35] in the country was Universalist Olympia Brown (1841–1926).[36] Born in Plymouth, Vermont, educated successively in Mount Holyoke, Antioch, and St. Lawrence Theological School, she was duly ordained by the Northern [New York] Universalist Association in Malone in 1863, despite the mild opposition of President Ebenezer Fisher. Olympia Brown had been instrumental in getting Antoinette Brown to speak and also to preach at Antioch—"I felt as though the Kingdom of Heaven were at hand."[37] It was at Antioch that Olympia planned to enter the ministry. Her daughter much later offered the view that the "ministry was the first objective of mother's life because of her belief that freedom of religious thought and a liberal church would supply the groundwork of other freedoms."[38]

Olympia Brown became a major figure in the women's suffrage movement. She had moved from the Weymouth pastorate in Massachusetts to Bridgeport, Connecticut, in 1870 and had the showman P. T. Barnum[39] among her admiring parishioners. Here she became a friend of Susan B. Anthony. Here she married and had her first child.[40] No other nationally prominent woman active in the American feminist movement from the 1860s would live to see the ratification of the Nineteenth Amendment to the Constitution in 1920 (significantly the sesquicentennial year of American Universalism).

Universalists counted many other women leaders, such as Phoebe A. Hanaford and Caroline A. Soule.[41] Their schools admitted women on an equal basis with men, Lombard College being second only to Oberlin in leading the way. Universalists into the twentieth century continued to be concerned with women and their rights.[42]

One of the most renowned names in the ranks of Universalist women is that of Clara Barton (1882–1912),[43] founder of the American Red Cross. Although never a member of a church, and in her later life also interested in spiritualism and Christian Science, she nevertheless continued throughout her career to identify herself with the denomination with which she had such powerful childhood associations. Her hometown of Oxford, Massachusetts, has been the site of the first permanent New England Convention of Universalists, called by John Murray in 1793; and she (incorrectly) believed that her father had been present at the ordination of Hosea Ballou, solemnized at the convention there in the following year.[44] She wrote,

> I was born to liberal views and have lived a liberal creed. I firmly believe in the divinity of Jesus Christ, the Jesus of Nazareth; in His life and death of suffering to save the world from sin, so far in His power to do. But it would be difficult for me to stop there and believe that this spark of divinity was accorded to none other of God's creation, who like the Master, took on the living form, and like Him, lived the human life.[45]

Such a Christlike spark of divinity, which she found in other feminine leaders of the time such as Julia Ward Howe, formed a part of her own imperious self-image.[46] Having been trained at the Clinton Liberal Institute (Universalist) in Clinton, New York, she taught in Bordentown, New Jersey, opening the school to all free of tuition (1852) and enlarging it to the point where a male principal was called, upon which she resigned, taking a position in the Patent Office in Washington. Her volunteer work in the Civil War, raising and directing supplies, and afterward in search of missing soldiers, was similarly independent of all organizations. Her extended tour of Europe, begun in 1869 as a remedy for nervous exhaustion, brought her into contact with the International Red Cross of Geneva during the Franco-Prussian War. The failure of the United States to ratify the Geneva Convention and begin a Red Cross agency had been the target of the Unitarian minister Henry Whitney Bellows for some years. He having failed, Miss Barton was commissioned to begin the U.S. Red Cross, which she did in 1881, achieving in the following year the United States' ratification of the Geneva Convention as well.[47]

Despite the early stand against discrimination toward women in the ministry and work of the denomination,[48] the Universalists maintained an ambivalent attitude toward the political enfranchisement of women. The Reverend Olympia Brown, who had been involved with Susan B. Anthony, Frederick Douglass, and others in the formation of an "Equal Rights Association" on behalf of both women and Negroes, in 1868 separated the two issues and organized the first Woman's Suffrage Association (for New England) with the help of such radicals as Adin Ballou and William Lloyd Garrison. The New England Association was followed the next year by the national organization. Her ministry in Racine, Wisconsin, included periodic campaigns and court battles for the right to vote.[49] Occasionally a minister like Erasmus Manford of St. Louis would come out for a woman for President if she could garner the votes. But only in 1905 did her denomination in general convention affirm "that the democratic ideal, the logic of our faith, and the interests of humanity demand that women be admitted to equal suffrage with men."[50] There was always a counter-current that seems to have stemmed from concern with the preservation of the traditional family structure and its values which appears in other resolutions of the time, such as those lamenting the increase in divorce and recommending uniform laws for its regulation, those urging the religious education of children, etc.[51] The strong paternal imagery in the denomination (as in the widespread use of the name, Church of the Divine Paternity, the common reference well into the twentieth century to "Father Murray," "Father Ballou," and "Father Shinn" and the widespread use of the appellation "Brother" and less frequently "Sister"—in common with Baptists and Methodists but in contrast to Unitarians) may have fed this countercurrent. In any case, a majority of convention delegates in succeeding years took the position adopted by Greeley: social reform benefiting women, but no national enfranchisement. In 1907 the resolution introduced by the Reverend Henrietta G. Moore of Ohio on women's suffrage was narrowly defeated (76 to 68),[52] and that of Henry H. Metcalf of New Hampshire in 1909 was simply tabled.[53] Metcalf emphasized the importance of putting into practice the Universalist and scriptural principle that there is in Christ neither male nor female and connected greater power for women with the whole range of typically Universalist social concerns:

> We believe in the refining and elevating influence of woman, not as an abstraction, but as a practical and positive power for good, a mighty agency for establishing the Kingdom of God among men. Therefore, to the end that the political life of municipality, state, and nation, may be purified, strengthened, and ennobled, the cause of temperance promoted, class privilege abolished, the war spirit discouraged, and equal and exact justice established, we favor the political enfranchisement of women throughout the country.[54]

This resolution of 1911 was also defeated (74 to 59). Nonetheless, within the denomination women continued to play a prominent role and gradually to assume more of the leadership positions.

TEMPERANCE AND THE WORKING CLASS

Despite such prophetic voices as those of Adin Ballou and Horace Greeley against wage slavery as an abomination no less than chattel slavery, most Universalists in the last third of the nineteenth century and beyond tended to think of labor and capital in moralistic terms; and there is some evidence, indeed, that the benign paternity of the heavenly Father and industrial paternalism were occasionally interrelated in the Universalist conception of stewardship, the more so for the reason that there was a strong fraternal and even communitarian ethos in Universalism.

The Universalist opposition to alcohol, for example, was moralistic and strongly tinged with concern for the moral uplift of the laboring classes. Quillen Shinn, from his Civil War experience and his work with persons of all ages and conditions, was opposed to both tobacco and liquor. In 1882 he presented a resolution against the use of wine at communion,[55] which was tabled with reference to the resolution of 1878. This earlier resolution, which was in force for the General Convention usage and advisory for the state conventions and local parishes,[56] placed the Universalist opposition to alcoholic beverages in the larger context of concern for the working class families and the more vulnerable sectors of society:

> Whereas, it is a self-evident fact that the use of intoxicating liquors is the curse of our country, filling our prisons with criminals, our poor-houses with paupers, our homes with sadness and mourning, destroying families, homes and affections, and is the one great obstacle to the better dissemination of Christian principles, therefore [be it]
>
> Resolved, that we will in all lawful ways discountenance its use in communion and recommend to the preachers of our faith everywhere that they by precept as well as example endeavor to rid the world of this blighting curse.[57]

In 1885 the Universalists celebrated a "Century of Temperance Reform," as having been inaugurated by the antialcoholic tract, *An Enquiry into the Effects of Spirituous Liquors upon the Human Body, and Their Influence Upon the Happiness of Society* (1784)[58] by the denominationally eclectic Dr. Benjamin Rush (1745–1813) of Philadelphia, signer of the Declaration of Independence, physician, and pioneer in the organization of the Philadelphia Universalist Convention of 1790 (claimed also by Episcopalians, Presbyterians, and Unitarians). The centennial resolution proclaimed "the duty of Prohibition by municipality, State and Nation."[59] After a slight subsidence of interest in temperance reform, Universalists, after 1919, called for enforcement of and obedience to the Eighteenth Amendment.[60] While it is true that tracts by Dr. Rush had a direct effect on the organization of the earliest temperance societies,[61] his later Universalist followers might have done well to note that he recommended the substitution of beer and wine for harder spirits. They might also read his delightful letter to John Adams[62] in which he recounts a dream of becoming President himself, foolishly prohibiting liquor, and failing entirely to change the habits of the people!

Dr. Rush, a pioneer in the organization of the Society for the Abolition of Slavery, and the other members of the Philadelphia convention of 1790 had also set the pattern for the interpretation of Universalism as demanding the abolition of economic and social bondage. They wrote:

> We believe it to be inconsistent with the union of the human race in a common Savior, and the obligations to mutual and universal love, which flow from that union, to hold any part of our fellow creatures in bondage. We therefore recommend a total refraining from the African trade and the adoption of prudent measures for the gradual abolition of the slavery of the negroes in our country, and for the instruction and education of their children in English literature, and in the principles of the Gospel.[63]

Rush, who had advanced a similar plan in his *Address ... upon Slavekeeping* (1773), himself financed and supported efforts to establish an African Church in Philadelphia and to set up freedmen as independent farmers in Pennsylvania. In 1795 he served as president of the National Convention of Abolition Societies.[64] Elhanan Winchester preached against slavery to his white congregations in South Carolina 1774–1793, and he worked devotedly among the slaves,[65] publishing *The Reigning Abominations, Especially the Slave Trade, Considered as Causes of Lamentations* (1788). Universalists as a whole, however, were no more in the forefront of the antislavery movement than other denominations in the early nineteenth century. When Adin Ballou adopted his radical abolitionist stand in 1837, many of his parishioners in Mendon, Massachusetts, left. Few at the time could recognize in him a notable exponent, over against alike the "antinomian" Garrisonians and the Liberty Party men and the main body of compromising clergy, of "the dialectical complexity" in emanicipation history, "who in all his humility [and communitarian separateness and perfectionism] had not rejected the notion that it was a human obligation to work out peaceful escapes from slavery and to foreshadow the kingdom of God."[66] The sectional conflicts leading to the Mexican War brought the General Convention of 1843 at Akron (which included no southern delegates) to adopt an antislavery resolution.[67] In 1845 a stronger manifesto alleging nine theological–ethical arguments against slavery was initiated by the Massachusetts Universalists and widely endorsed.[68]

In the course of the nineteenth century, the focus of reformist economic and social concern shifted from opposition to slavery to the economic integration of the freedmen and to the economic enfranchisement of industrial workers and others in the growing cities and mill towns. Universalism, as the product of rural society, did not respond comfortably to the new needs of industrial workers, so many of whom were foreign-born and Catholic. They were often disposed to foster the paternalism of many businessmen as Christian charity and stewardship, while calling for workingmen to turn to Christ as a source of self-restraint and improvement.[69]

Universalists were especially responsive to the exploitation of women and children by industry. In Lowell, Massachusetts, considered at the time a model city for the humane treatment of young women working in the textile mills, the Universalists were represented from 1832 to 1845 by the Reverend Abel C. Thomas (1807–1880), of Quaker heritage; and the Reverend Thomas Baldwin Thayer (1812–1886) destined to become a major Universalist theologian,[70] who organized "Improvement Circles" and publications such as *The Star of Bethlehem* (1841–1842) and *The Lowell Offering* to provide a degree of educational refinement for working women.[71] Massachusetts Universalists, on the initiative of the Reverend C. H. Fay in Roxbury, created a general reform association for social responsibility which functioned from 1846 to 1863.[72] A number of Universalists took an important role in securing laws against child labor.[73]

After the Civil War the whole cluster of Universalist humanitarian concerns surfaced in the General Convention at Peoria in 1884 in the following resolution by Amos Crum of Iowa:

> That the Universalist General Convention . . . recommends . . . an increased attention to the great humanitarian problems of the world. It proclaims its world-wide sympathy with poor, unfortunate, struggling humanity. It further urges upon all members of its faith and fellowship a practical co-operation with all movements and purposes for the prevention of cruelty to children and animals, and for the removal of the causes thereof.[74]

The most revealing episode among Universalist reactions to labor problems in the late nineteenth century came a decade later with the Pullman Strike in Chicago of 1894. On the day before the strike began, a sermon by the Reverend Levi M. Powers, the leading Universalist advocate of greater economic equality through a moderate socialism, stated,

> ... when you permit one man to possess one hundred millions of wealth, as several men in this country do, you give into his care and merciful, or rather merciless, keeping just seventy-five thousand slaves, with this disadvantage, that the slaves of today are mocked with a seeming freedom which they do not have, and the man who owns them, doesn't know he owns them and so feels no responsibility to keep them from starvation or care for them in sickness.[75]

Going beyond the condemnation of greed,[76] Powers pointed out some of the inherent difficulties of industrial paternalism, of which a leading representative was George Mortimer Pullman (d. 1897), founder of the Pullman Palace Car Company, Universalist layman, and brother of two Universalist ministers, the Reverend Royal Henry Pullman (1826–1900),[77] and the Reverend James Minton Pullman (1836–1903).[78] The company town of Pullman, Illinois (now a part of Chicago), was the site of an experiment in paternalistic industrial order and community planning.[79] It was also, alas, the scene of the most notorious labor dispute of the time, begun when Pullman, under the deflationary pressure of the Panic of 1893, reduced his employees' wages by twenty-five percent, while maintaining rents and fees on the company-owned houses (and churches!) at the same level. He refused to recognize collective bargaining or arbitration, claiming that any other arrangement would force him to close the plant. His refusal resulted in the boycott of Pullman cars by the American Railway Union, under Eugene V. Debs, in support of the Pullman workers.[80]

The reaction of the Universalist press was even more antilabor in this instance than the national press at large, especially when violence broke out and troops were sent in to deliver the mails.[81] In the midst of the strike, The Pullman Memorial Church near the Pullman homestead at Albion, New York, was dedicated.[82] The Reverend Charles H. Eaton of the Church of the Divine Paternity in New York City, another Pullman relation, offered the prayer.[83] *The Christian*

Leader not only took the part of industrialist George Pullman, supporting in its editorial comments[84] his refusal to go to arbitration, but also published Eaton's address on Pullman's character,[85] in which he asserted that "the town of Pullman is sympathy embodied" and alluded to the socioeconomic implications for an industrial society of the Universalist doctrine of the divine paternity. Charles Eaton's life-long support of business, Republicanism, and the gold standard,[86] seems to have been grounded in a source even more interesting than his kinship to industrialist Pullman. His ministerial training had been at the hands of Eben Draper, one of the original members of the Hopedale Community, and father of the General Draper who terminated the communitarian industrial experiment and converted it into a conventional capitalistic machine-manufacturing enterprise. It was the apparent failure of Adin Ballou's socialism and the success of Draper's capitalistic paternalism that powerfully influenced Eaton's later social and political views.[87] Eaton's remarks to the Chicago General Convention of 1897 on the sudden death of George Pullman (whose houseguest he had been) show his tendency to identify Christian American paternalistic industrialism with rural, Jeffersonian democracy and small-town enterprise:

> Democracy is not mobocracy [in allusion to Mr. Pullman's recent labor troubles]; not the undermining of existing institutions. A false democracy has drunk of anarchism and law has been forgotten in the drivel of what is base. The Universalist church is the child of the people; came up out of the soil, and industry has crowned her if she should be crowned at all.[88]

A more theological defense of paternalism came from the Reverend James M. Pullman, who based it on the "Universalist doctrine of the mutual responsibility of moral beings," going on to say,

> Between moral beings there can be no obligation on one side without obligation on the other. And the measure of that obligation is power. It is by this doctrine, and this only, that class-antagonisms can be reconciled, and the spirit of warfare between the workman and the employer be quenched. The strongest party has the larger responsibility, and is under the higher obligation.[89]

Over against the industrialist paternalism of the very influential Universalist Pullman family, there were the words and actions of such Universalist stalwarts as the Reverend Legrand Powers who served as labor commissioner of Minnesota from 1891 to 1898, of the ranking Bible scholar Orello Cone of Buchtel and St. Lawrence with his *Rich and Poor in the New Testament* (1902), and the already cited Reverend Levi M. Powers. In 1900, linking capitalistic exploitation at home and imperial–economic expansion in the Philippines, Levi Powers was mordant, contrasting American society as it was with the Republic of God:

> The Republic of the United States believes that three hundred thousand men should ask another man for the right to live and work— that those who come late should pay the children of those who come early for a chance to live on the footstool of the Most High, that some men have a right by law to compel others to contribute to their success. The Republic of the United States seems now to believe that the people of the Islands of the Seas must ask us to give them whatever measure of liberty we think wise. In the Republic of God, which it is our business to establish here, the very thought of one nation being subject to another or of one person living upon the labor of another will be impossible.[90]

The approach of Universalists to labor, immigrant, and imperialist problems was thus diversified. But for the most part their humanitarian sensibilities were more inclined to a moralistic and sentimental rather than political and trade unionist approach. Thus the prevailing Universalist stress in periodical, pulpit, and parish was on charitable relief and social service even after the establishment of the new Universalist Commission on Social Service under the Reverend Frank O. Hall in 1909.[91]

The outbreak of war in Europe in 1914 accelerated the social and economic processes in the United States and diversified the range of social theory in and outside the various denominations, many of them well caught up by the social gospel. Clarence R. Skinner (see further below at pages 75-78), after his appointment to the chair of Applied Christianity at Crane Theological School in 1914, serialized in *The Universalist Leader* in 1915 his programmatic lectures at

Tufts as "The Social Implications of Universalism," which proved very influential in the denomination.[92] In 1917 the denomination's doctrinal predisposition against the conservative social Darwinism (i.e., the economic and social survival of the fittest competitor) of the late nineteenth century was well articulated in "A Declaration of Social Principles":

> [W]e hold it to be self-evident that mankind is led into sin by evil surroundings, by the evils of unjust social and economic conditions [rather than "by inherent depravity"]. . . . While cooperating to the fullest extent possible with the various forms of charity, relief, and correction, we recognize that they do not eradicate fundamental causes. We would mobilize the forces of our church against the causes which create misery, disease, accidents, ignorance, and crime, and summon all our strength to the establishment of justice, education, and social righteousness.
>
> Some form of social insurance should gradually replace the present individualistic and inadequate methods of charitable relief.[93]

The Declaration made bold even to claim that "the Universalist Church offers a complete program for completing humanity":

1. An Economic Order which shall give to every human being an equal share in the common gifts of God, and in addition all that he shall earn by his own labor.
2. A Social Order in which there shall be equal rights for all, special privilege for none, the help of the strong for the weak until the weak become strong.
3. A Moral Order in which all human law and action shall be the expression of the moral order of the universe.
4. A Spiritual Order which shall build out of the growing lives of living men the growing temple of the living God.[94]

After the war, a new type of industrial leader emerged among Universalists, Owen D. Young (1874–1962), nurtured by, and ever loyal to, the Universalist Church of his native Van Hornesville, New York, and a graduate and life-long benefactor of the St. Lawrence University (1894). Young, chairman of the board of General Electric (1922–1944), served on the committee arranging for Germany's payment of reparations (1920–1930). He, very early in his career, recognized labor's right of collective bargaining.[95]

On the side of organizing and then organized labor itself and roughly a contemporary of Young and almost exactly coeval with Dean Skinner (1881–1949) in academe was the Universalist pacifist, socialist, minister, and impassioned labor leader Henry Clay Ledyard (1880–1950), who in a notable address in San Diego in 1921 declared, "Today organized labor is preaching good news to the poor and industrial freedom to the wage slave."[96]

PENAL REFORM, CAPITAL PUNISHMENT, AND SPIRITUALISM

Universalists were prominent in penal reform and much concerned with the abolition of capital punishment and with the humane treatment of criminals, animals, and children. The interest was, of course, part of a general upsurge of humanitarianism during the nineteenth century, expressed in the formation of numerous eleemosynary and reform societies of all kinds. But the Universalist interest had also distinctive denominational sanction and motivation. In general, it can be said that the Universalist elimination of endless punishment in hell and the interpretation of suffering beyond the grave as purifactory rather than punitive worked steadily upon Universalists, leading them to help bring the earthly penal systems into accord with their larger understanding of the proper purpose of chastisement. Then, too, the fact that the Father of American Universalism had himself been thrown into debtor's prison in London, that he had himself, as recorded in his oft-printed autobiography, chosen to preach to prisoners, for example, in Newport and in Philadelphia, where he was notably affected by the extreme penalty of death meted out, and that in his final paralysis in Boston he chose to call himself "the Lord's prisoner," "a prisoner of hope,"[97] all tended to sensitize his followers to the needs of prisoners and to the reform of penology. It is possible, also, that Murray's strong feeling for the beauties and harmonies of nature, his belief in the restitution and final harmony of all things, including the assuagement of cruelties done to animals,[98] contributed to recurrent Universalist sensibility in this sector. Universalists

51

themselves were quite explicit about the connection between their distinctive views of predestination, atonement, and penology.

Dr. John G. Adams, looking back at Universalist reform movements from the vantage point of 1881, for example, could see a connection between Universalist doctrine and penal reform over against the influence in that sector of the Calvinist doctrine of the total depravity of man and limited atonement:

> The time is generally more in accordance with these [humane] considerations than in the past, when severity was deemed more needful as applied to criminals who were subjects of total depravity, than a proportionate mercy, which regarded them not only as lost ones, hut as capable of a possible restoration to their rightful Owner and Almighty Friend.[99]

Likewise, Quillen Shinn, introducing in 1900 an essay on capital punishment in an anthology of summer conference lectures, declared, "A church having for its foundation the law of love, which returns good for evil, will not have discharged its full duty until the death penalty is abolished."[100] Finally, the Reverend Levi M. Powers, looking back from the sesquicentennial period in 1920, could again appropriately declare, "The Universalist Church has always been a leader in Prison Reform. With our idea of the nature of punishment this was inevitable."[101]

In 1882 the Reverend George Washington Quinby (1810–1884) of Maine, long a student of the relationship between poverty and crime and author of *The Gallows, the Prison, and the Poor House: A Plea for Humanity, Showing the Demands of Christianity in Behalf of the Criminal and Perishing Classes* (1856), introduced in general convention the following resolution, unanimously adopted:

> Whereas, in the sense of this Convention, the Death Penalty is barbarous, revolting, demoralizing, contrary to the spirit of the Christian Religion, and unnecessary; therefore, resolved, that we commend all proper efforts for its abolishment in all our States, and recommend that a more humane and effective penalty be substituted.[102]

Quinby's campaign had effect in Maine, where the death penalty was abolished in 1887. His widow Cornelia A. Quinby, appointed by the governor as official visitor and then trustee, carried on the work in Maine by stimulating improvements in the asylum care of the insane.

The concern of the Quinbys and their associates in penal reform carried forward, as we have said, a venerable Universalist theme. In 1791, Dr. Benjamin Rush wrote,

> A belief in God's universal love to all his creatures, and that he will finally restore all those of them that are miserable to happiness, is a *polar* truth. It leads to truths upon all subjects, more especially upon the subject of government. It establishes the *equality* of mankind— it abolishes the punishment of death for any crime—and converts jails into houses of repentance and reformation.[103]

Thomas Whittemore, the ministerial historian of Universalism, editor, and financier, attacked capital punishment as early as 1828.[104]

One of the founders and long-time secretary of the Society for the Abolition of Capital Punishment had been Charles Spear (1801–1863), a student of Hosea Ballou, serving successively as pastor in Brewster, Rockport, and Boston. In his *Essays on the Punishment of Death* (1844), Spear began by quoting Dr. Rush on the sacredness of human life. With his brother, John Murray Spear (1804–1887), he published the prison reform journal, *The Hangman,* then *The Prisoner's Friend* (1845–1859), in which he serialized articles later published in *A Plea for Discharged Convicts* (1846). Charles Spear died ministering to the Civil War wounded. His brother carried out his lonely mission of ministering for years to the prisoners in and around Boston."[105]

It is of interest and quite in accord with the correlation we have noted between Universalist reformed penology and theory of the limited punishment in the afterlife that several penal reformers at mid-century were also particularly fascinated by spiritualism and communication with those who were presumably experiencing chastisement or beatitude in the afterlife.[106] John Murray Spear was himself a medium. His successor in the pulpit at Weymouth, Massachusetts, Olympia Brown, who was also opposed to capital punishment,[107] attended seances, but was highly skeptical.[108] In the summer of 1852 Spear gave a series of lectures while in a trance, purportedly bringing *Messages from the Superior State* communicated by (his namesake) John Murray.[109] Similarly, Adin Ballou published *An Exposition of Views Respecting the Principal Facts, Causes, and Peculiarities Involved in Spirit Manifestations* (1852). The following year Orestes Brownson, the former Universalist minister, now a Catholic, mordantly attacked the phenomenon of spiritualism.[110] In the *Messages* to Spear, there was an appeal to the young hearer or reader to escape the prison of the institutional church and to read the book of nature. John Murray Spear himself ended his life in a pacifist community, "Spiritual Springs," on the New York–Pennsylvania border.[111] Even Clara Barton was attracted by Spiritualism, and seemingly, though not through a medium, had facile contact with several other notables including Lincoln and Theodore Parker.[112]

Unlike Charles Spear, Clara Barton survived her ministry in the Civil War hospitals and prison camps to make also her mark on penal reform, serving briefly (1884) as the superintendent of the Women's Reformatory Prison at Sherburne, Massachusetts, where she was succeeded by still another Universalist woman, Mrs. Ellen C. Jackson. Mrs. Jackson served more than fifteen years in that position, making an impact on the treatment of women prisoners parallel to that of her fellow Universalist, Thomas Mott Osborne (1859–1926). Osborne's long and humane, though controversial, tenure as the superintendent of Sing-Sing resulted in the improvement of the parole and rehabilitation systems there and beyond his jurisdiction. Osborne's contemporary and associate Orlando Lewis (1873–1922), sociologist and general secretary of the Prison Association of New York, was noted for his work, *The Development of American Prisons and Prison Customs, 1776–1845* (1922).[113] Mrs. Jackson, following her death in 1899, was eulogized in a resolution introduced by Quillen H. Shinn, the head of the General Convention's committee on penology (established four year previously). He noted that she had "succeeded in reaching the mother nature in the most refractory women under her care," and urged that the fourth Sunday of October be observed as Prison Sunday in all Universalist churches.[114] There is an echo of the Universalist concern with the elimination of endless punishment in the hereafter and penal reform in Shinn's comments about this time on the National Prison Congress held at Indianapolis. Writing for his column in the denominational press,[115] he declared that among the prison reformers "over and over, from begining to end, the great principle of Universalism was insisted upon, namely, that punishment is not to satisfy justice or vindicate the law, but to cure the criminal." The religious conviction, going beyond Calvinism, that man is "wicked but not worthless" was seen as being directly connected with the reformatory principle that "there are no incorrigibles." He quoted another participant in the conference[116] as to the correlative effect of the philosophy of prison reform on theology, namely, that it gave "the death blow to the doctrine of endless torment."

WAR, PEACE, AND CONSCIENCE

One of the strongest and most consistent social concerns of Universalist General Conventions in the second century of the denomination's history was the evil of war. At the Centennial Convention in 1870 resolutions on "the importance of settling all international disputes by arbitration or a national congress" were introduced by the Reverend Eli Ballou of Vermont, but due to the lateness of the hour on the final day of the assembly, they were deferred for rewording until the next year.[117] A similar proposal introduced by the Reverend L. J. Fletcher of New York at the General Convention of 1875 in Lynn was adopted unanimously.[118] The Universalist position on arbitration was reiterated in the Reverend Alonzo A. Miner's resolution at Brooklyn[119] in 1885 and by others.[120] In 1892, the Universalists sent a delegation to an interdenominational conference on peace and arbitration at the Columbian Exposition in Chicago, and memorialized thirty-one governments on the subject.[121] In accepting the invitation in 1905 of the American Unitarian Association to participate in the International Congress of Religious Liberals (which evolved into the International Association for Religious Freedom), to meet in Boston in 1907, Universalists joined hands for the purpose of establishing "the Fraternity of Nations, Brotherhood of Mankind, and Peace of the World."[122]

The selection of arbitration as the consensual position of the denomination in the face of the endemic problem of violent human conflict represents primarily the expression of what we have designated the dominant "Christian Universalism" of the Centennial, which had pushed the pacifistic restorationist eschatologically oriented sectarianism of Adin Ballou to the fringes of the denomination or into the denominational subconscious. The denominational interest in arbitration represented also a compromise between the interpretation of Universalism as the religion of American democracy and the interpretation of itself as a world religion.

Such a tension in the Universalist interpretation of the Christian peace ethic, between the demands of the American democracy and the desire to implement the Kingdom of Universal World Peace through the action of the individual conscience and on the model of the early Church, was notable in the immediate post-Revolutionary era of Universalism, as it was again in the post–Civil War period and after World War I. The position of men like Dr. Rush, despite his sympathy with Quaker pacifism and conscientious objection to participation in warfare, had led the Philadelphia Universalist Convention of 1790 to adopt the following recommendation "Of War":

> Although a defensive war may be considered lawful, yet we believe there is a time coming, when the light and universal love of the gospel, shall put an end to all wars. We recommend, therefore, to all churches in our communion, to cultivate the spirit of peace and brotherly love, which shall lead them to consider all mankind as brethren, and to strive to spread among them the knowledge of their Saviour and Redeemer, who came into the world "not to destroy men's lives, but to save them.[123]

The principal Universalist pacifist between revolution and civil war, Adin Ballou, had the virtue of keeping alive, with a few others, the witness of radical Christian pacifism, or "non-resistance."[124] By his own account, his social views were originally inspired by other reformers, rather than by his Universalist faith. The identification of Universalism with American democratic patriotism is evident in his early ministry: his service as a militia chaplain (like John Murray in the Revolution), his membership in the Freemasons, and two important orations on the Fourth of July.[125] "Patriotism—civil, military, and religious—was then an essential part of my Christianity," he said,[126] and blamed this attitude for his earlier blindness to the injustices of slavery.[127] By 1838, however, his contact with radical Abolitionists, such as William Lloyd Garrison, had interested Adin Ballou in one of their other organizations as well, the New England Non-Resistance Society.[128] Finding pacifism consonant with the New Testament ethical injunction "resist not evil" (Matthew 5:39), Ballou carried it out in *Christian Non-Resistance* (1846) with the relentless logic that characterized all his thought. (His book would eventually deeply impress Count Leo Tolstoy, with whom at the end of his life he entered into correspondence.)[129] Violence, even in self-defense or in defense of others, was excluded from Ballou's form of Christian nonresistance, as was collaboration in any way with persons or institutions prepared to use capital force. Thus participation in government, by voting or holding office, could not be condoned so long as that government was prepared to wage war or exact the death penalty.[130] Ballou's theological basis for this position forms a unique interpretation of Christian Restorationism. He had, from the moment of his entry into Universalist fellowship,[131] differed with those "ultra-Universalists" or "Death and Glory Universalists" who denied all punishment in the afterlife, taking the Restorationist position that in the millennium prelapsarian blessedness and peace could be restored only after suitable individualized chastisement. Such Restorationism affected Ballou's matured peace ethics in two ways. Not only did he now take the "immediatist" position that sought for the application in the here-and-now of the "principles, dispositions, and moral obligations of . . . the millennium," seen as identical with a perfectionist view of New Testament ethics[132]; but also he understood such perfectionism as the restoration of primitive Christian purity.[133]

During the Mexican War of 1845–1848, which brought many antislavery people into the antiwar and pacifist fold, this latter position was taken by another Universalist radical pacifist of the time, the Reverend John Gregory of Vermont, addressing the Vermont Convention there in 1846:

> Brethren, no one can be more anxious for the spread of Universalism than your speaker. But I want such kind of Universalism to prevail as triumphed during the three hundred years after Christ. The

Universalism during that period would not allow its believers to fight, even in self-defense. No Christian, and all were Universalists during that time, generally speaking, would take up arms against another. To the solicitations of all who endeavored to enlist them under the God of battles, the same God who presides over battles at the present day, the reply was, "We are Christians and cannot fight." O! that it might be said of modern Universalists, "They are Chrisians and cannot fight." Then our Universalism would be worth having. It would, in truth, be good for something. But the Universalism in our day, has so much Partialism in it, that men might almost as well be Partialists as Universalists.[134]

It is noteworthy that the Universalist self-image allowed at this date the state convention to think of the whole of pre-Constantinian Christianity as Universalist! Yet, as Gregory indicates, very few of his contemporary Universalists actually took a pacifist position. The Mexican War, however, did provide the occasion for the organization of the Universalist General Reform Association, dedicated to fight "war, intemperance, slavery, and capital punishment,"[135] but an increasing tendency to identify the denomination as the religion of the righteous Republic precluded a collectively pacifist position. Although John Gregory felt that the Universalist stand should be that of the Quakers,[136] the bulk of the denomination, despite the earlier identification with primitive Christianity inside the bellicose Roman Empire, was uneasy about any outright pacifism (as likewise were the Unitarians); and the abolitionists in the denomination became impatient with their erstwhile pacifist allies as civil war impended.[137]

Likewise most Universalists seem to have identified themselves with the democratic ideals of the Cuban Revolution in countenancing the Spanish-American War.[138] Later they endorsed the idealized purposes of the First World War, resolving in general convention in 1917 "complete devotion to the American Ideals" and pledging their "loyal support in making this world safe for democracy."[139] The resolution did not go without debate,[140] but the majority of the delegates probably agreed with the occasional preacher of the Convention, the Reverend Henry R. Rose of Newark, who felt that he, in the defense of democracy, was "right as a Christian to be on the side of our soldiers instead of our professional pacifists."[141] Since the Universalists gave no official status to conscientious objectors, a number of Universalist laymen suffered under the law, as did pacifist Universalist ministers under public opinion.[142]

Throughout the 1920s the ideal of transforming America into the righteous nation, seen in resolutions calling for obedience to Prohibition and law, as well as new uncertainty about the future of Universalism,[143] did not allow the question of conscientious objection to surface. Only with the furor over the threatened deportation of immigrant pacifist Douglas Macintosh in 1931 did the General Convention adopt, for this special sector of public life, a statement endorsing the "supremacy of conscience."[144] Provision was made that "fellowship in this Convention shall confer the right to interpret the general purpose and spirit of the Universalist faith as sanctioning refusing of all forms of military service, if such refusal be based on conscientious grounds,"[145] but no certainty of legal protection was reached until the Second World War.[146]

OUR WORD AND WORK FOR MISSIONS ABROAD[147]

By 1882 Universalists in Massachusetts, who had long thought of their faith as a means of Protestant reformation or social benevolence, hailed, in convention assembled, "the rising spirit among our people in favor of foreign missions . . . as a favorable indication of a deeper sense of responsibility for the salvation of the world."[148] It had been an address by Dr. Thomas Baldwin Thayer on foreign missions that prompted the approbation and the collection of the first offering for this purpose in Universalist history. At the General Convention the following month at Philadelphia, Universalists were nationally prepared to say, "The time has come for our Church to look toward the establishment of missions in heathen lands."[149]

Scout for the most appropriate terrain for a foreign mission was the Reverend James Henry Chapin (1832–1892), who as the agent of the Massachusetts Universalist Convention, had been the organizer of the Centennial of 1870. A graduate of Lombard College in Illinois, with a life-long interest in geology, agent for the Civil War

Sanitary Commission in the crucial state of California, and secretary of the New England Freedman's Aid Commission, Chapin was a man accustomed to cooperate with other Christians in great causes.[150] After the Centennial, he became a professor of geology and mineralogy at St. Lawrence University and in 1873 accepted a call to a pastorate in Meriden, Connecticut, while retaining his professorship at Canton on the basis of giving lectures there for six weeks every spring. In this capacity he wrote a book that combined his interests in geology and sociology, *The Creation and the Early Development of Society* (1880). It was in 1875 that Dr.[151] Chapin set forth in a sermon the theme that was to give special significance to the last phase of his career. In his published sermon *The Keys of the Kingdom of Heaven,* based on Matthew 16:19, he proclaimed "that the same commission [as that to Peter] is given to everyone that bears the Christian name."[152] In 1887 Dr. Chapin was called by the General Convention as its agent for studying the possibility of making Japan a major center for the Universalist mission abroad.[153]

While the idea of launching a Universalist mission was preparing itself, the Universalists in general convention in Akron in 1886 characteristically combined their humanitarian and religious concerns in passing unanimously an extended resolution that criticized Christian nations collectively and their citizens individually in the treatment of pagan peoples abroad and at home (Native Americans, Asian immigrants, etc.). Notable was the convention's expression of abhorrence at "the barbarities practiced by certain of the citizens of this Christian land against the Chinese at Rock Springs and Seattle ...," involving the serious loss of life. The convention demanded that reparations be paid, going on to assert that "the interest of our common Christianity suffers incalculable harm in the minds of pagan countries from the wrongs committed ... by Christian people against them."[154] The resolution introduced by Dr. E. L. Rexford, then of Detroit, referred especially to the injustices and crudities of the English in India and China ("if England should ever leave India, she would leave as among her chief memorials, mountains of empty beer bottles and half-smoked cigars"). Convinced that "rational and practical Christianity can be vastly enhanced, both in our own minds and those of foreign peoples, by a radical and far-reaching reform, and by abandonment of great evils that still linger in our midst," the convention in the same resolution also had this to say against abortion:

> That while we deplore the superstition of African mothers, who sacrifice their children by casting them to the crocodiles in appeasement of the hungry gods, we deplore the vastly multiplied crime of Christian mothers of Europe and America, taking the form of *infanticide,* whose records in the medical literature of Europe and America appall the lingering sense of humanity in our midst.[155]

The idea of a foreign mission to the heathen was still not easy for Universalists to accept. As the idea broached in 1882 took shape in 1890 (with Universalists at their peak: 50,000) as a mission to Japan, *The Christian Leader* in "Concerning Our New Enterprise" editorialized, "Twenty-five years ago a Foreign Mission by the Universalist Church . . . had no champions and but few sympathizers among Universalists." Fully approving, however, of the venture on a trial basis, the editorial looked back at the more familiar process of universalizing Protestantism in America:

> [T]hus far our converts have been made out of Orthodox timber. . . . Must human nature be "Orthodoxized"—if such a term may be coined—as a prerequisite to its being "Universalized?" For ought we *by experiment* know to the contrary, such *may* be our limitations, and our logical relation to Orthodoxy. . . . Shoes are not made of hides but of leather. The raw skin must be tanned. . . . Must human souls have an Orthodox tanning before they can be vamped or shaped into Universalist believers and workers?[156]

With much more than spiritual cobbling in mind, a Universalist missionary band of three reached Japan in April 1890. One of them, Dr. George Landor Perin, interpreting this event and the achievement to date in September 1893, explained before the Universalist Congress in Chicago (part of the World's Parliament of Religions) that Universalists had been not at the start engaged in a foreign mission because, like that of Martin Luther, their first task had been a reformation of traditional Christianity but that now that their "central idea has found wide acceptance in the Episcopal church, and as a hope at least among Congregationalists and other churches," Universalists were at length at liberty to turn from reformation to foreign missions.[157] "A Universalist without the missionary spirit," he would even be bold now to say, "is a contradiction in terms. Such a one suggests the idea of partial Universalism."[158] He acknowledged that Universalists had not the same motivation as that of all other Christian missionaries, for they could not hold that the heathen were in any danger of eternal torment for want of a direct knowledge of Christ, and Universalists were confident of the invisible efficacy and "the Universal character of Christ's atonement."[159] But Perin knew that there was much to be brought to the heathen by way of Christian culture in the present life. Eschewing any direct intention of influencing abroad persons "already converted" in competition with other missionaries, and deploring the behavior and attitude "of a part of the numerous class of foreign residents, who have no other interest in the country or the people than to use them for their own pleasure or profit,"[160] Perin, with respect to Japan, was confident that it might indeed "become a Christian nation . . . through the preaching of a simple Christianity, freed from theological difficulties, in which the love of God for all men stands out clearly as the central message."[161] He understood Universalism to be "the most faultless evolution of theology the world has yet seen. It seems the freest from superstitions, the largest in aims, the completest in answers, the fullest and most accurate in its solutions of the difficult problems of the universe. It is to me, indeed, the very flower of Christianity."[162]

Dr. C. Ellwood Nash of Galesburg, Illinois, contemplating the possibilities for mission work of the Universalist Church, expressed the same thought in bluff speech:

We [Universalists] have the truth, the *real* gospel. We stand ready, and we feel qualified, to offer reassurance to minds rent by doubts; to unriddle much of life's most puzzling mystery; to give comfort, cheer, guidance, to all. Our faith is revelational; it is rational; it is inspirational; it is sunny, though serious; it harmonizes the providences of God and the faculties of man; it is democratic; it anticipates and allows for progress; it embodies the genius of the best age the world has had; it welcomes science, evolution, even revolution in its place, while religiously holding fast to the heritage of past uplifts. . . . Could any service be geater than to help to equip the world with such faith? . . . . That Universalism is such a faith as the world needs and is seeking I . . . have no doubt at all. . . . I confess that I do anticipate its ultimate acceptance as (in outline at any rate) *the universal religion.*[163]

We can hear in Nash in 1894 the Christian Transcendentalism that would lead to Clarence Skinner's Religion for Greatness in 1945.

Nash's fellow symposiast, Dr. Edwin C. Sweetser, however, holding to Christianity as the final universal religion, had preserved much more of scriptural and evangelical Christianity in his vision of Universalism in the global *oikoumene,* than Nash. He stressed its future role both among the American Indians in the Far West and in the East among the deracinated rural and immigrant denizens of booming cities:

> [T]he Christian religion shows unlimited adaptability and expansiveness. Wrapped up in the New Testament, it can be opened indefinitely, and will accommodate as few or as many as may be. It belongs to the Lord of hosts and the Father of all men. Families, communities, nations may rest in it. The whole world may be enfolded by it, and the indications are that it certainly will be. This cannot be said of any other religion. . . . Christianity [i.e., Christian Universalism] includes all the truth of other religions, excludes all their errors, supplements their *partial* truth with the further truth which human nature stands in need of . . . and sends it forth, conquering and to conquer, on its mission of salvation among all races of men. . . . For mankind stand in need of a personal Saviour. . . . Only in Christianity and in the person of Jesus does this need of humanity find satisfaction.[164]

It is notable, and pregnant with the future,[165] that Sweetser would here, perhaps quite unconsciously, apply the distinctively Universalist term *partial* for Calvinism, etc., to the world religions as also partial in contrast to (Universalist) Christianity.

A generation later a product of the Japanese mission would bring greetings to the sesquicentennial celebrants at Gloucester in 1920 and in answer to his own question "why does Japan need Christianity?" declare, "Nippon needs Universalism,"[166] because of Jesus' liberating words and actions with respect to women in civilization, because of the Universalist nurture of a "more natural and happy nature" than is usual among the Japanese, and because of the close link between Universalism and democracy. He concluded optimistically that with much greater support from America, "[s]hould we not make our religion [Universalism] the world religion for world service literally in the next half century?"

AGAIN THE NATURE AND DESTINY OF THE
UNIVERSALIST CHURCH (1890–1946): CHANGES IN UNIVERSALIST
THEOLOGY AS REFLECTED IN INTERFAITH ACTIVITY

Despite the extraordinary achievements of the denomination in the course of the nineteenth century with the confident expectation within (and, earlier at least, with the fear from without) that Universalism would emerge as a major expression of the American experience of and transformation of Christianity, the fact is that by the first decade of the twentieth century the feeling was abroad in the denomination that its original mission (reform) had been accomplished in other denominations and that the denomination might henceforth have to settle down like other programmatic Christians, such as the Campbellites, the Millerites, and the Mormons, to being just one more American denomination.[167] But, then, there was also the strong possibility of a fundamental reconception of Universalism, no longer in the context of Calvinism or even of Christian denominationalism but in the context of world religions.[168]

The Japanese convert to Universalist Christianity cited in the preceding section, in the euphoria of the sesquicentennial in 1920 could, perhaps somewhat rhetorically, think of American Universalism as the Religion for World Service. The very impulse that had belatedly induced Universalists to engage in a foreign mission of the usual Christian type had come out just thirty years later in the Japanese version of Universalism as something more than Christian. In other words, the forces impelling a Christian mission abroad turned out to carry with them the very energies that at home were driving the denomination toward an expanded understanding of Universalism that John Murray, Elhanan Winchester, and Hosea Ballou might not have immediately subsumed under their original concept of Universalism in their sense of universal as distinguished from partial atonement through Christ's obedient death.

It is useful, therefore, at this juncture to return to the concept of the Universalist Church which had been so prominent at the Centennial in 1870 to see what kind of thinking had evolved by the end of the century with respect to theology in general, but again with special reference to the Church as a clue to all the rest. It will be convenient, first to take up the changes in terms of Universalist attitudes toward rapprochement with the two other denominations of New England origin, Unitarian and Congregationalist. Then, we shall take up the transformation of Universalism as World Religion.

Relations With Unitarians, 1890–1917

In 1890 the Unitarians and Universalists began to draw together in fitful uncertainty as to how they actually felt toward one another. When Edward Everett Hale disclaimed any "innuendo" of denominational union at the Centennial,[169] he could not have been unaware of a Universalist sentiment like that of Moses Ballou (d. 1879), who had in 1860 written bitterly because of the seeming obliviousness on the part of Unitarians to Universalist contributions to liberalism, "I think that there is no sect on earth which would more gladly destroy us than the Unitarian, if it had but the power to do so."[170] And John Wesley Hanson had said as recently as 1867, though he could at the moment see "cheering signs" of change, "The Unitarians and Universalists have too long seemed to occupy semi-hostile attitudes. While the self-styled Evangelical sects . . . have united in solid phalanx against all liberal movements, we, the Siamese twins of progress, the two great and growing liberal sects, have stood aloof from each other and allowed the united armies of the alien to advance as they should not have done."[171] In 1872 a Unitarian, the Reverend Dr. George Putnam of Roxbury (Boston), though he acknowledged that the two "have always been working towards the same end," put his finger on "a difference in administration" as an explanation for the difficulties and reason enough for him, at least, not "to cry aloud for union."[172]

The effort at uniting the two denominations in the 1890s, either through inclusion in some much larger fellowship or council of liberal churches or through some kind of cooperation between just the two denominations in several degrees of proximity, got its primary impetus in the Chicago region, partly as a consequence of the greater openness to new ways in the West and partly as a direct consequence of the World's Parliament of Religions in 1893, but there were also efforts at approximation in New England and elsewhere. Besides the general stimulus to work for a world religion in the Chicago Parliament affecting transcendentalists in both denominations, there was from the Universalist side support for merger from an unexpected quarter, given the expressly Christian motivation in the mission to Japan, namely, that of Dr. Perin who urged a united liberal denomination in order to advance the liberal Christian mission in Japan and elsewhere.[173]

A western effort at cooperation was the Christian Alliance. Then under the inspiration of Unitarian Jenkin Lloyd Jones of All Souls Church in Chicago, who had headed as general secretary the Parliament in 1893, the First Congress of Liberal Religious Societies, embracing Universalists, Unitarians, Reform Jews, and Ethical Culturists, met in Sinai Temple in Chicago in May, 1894. *Unity*, edited by Jones, and now the organ of this new grouping, announced itself on the title page as "an advocate of Universal religion and a co-worker with all free churches." Jones, distinguishing at least two groups in Universalism, commended the more liberal "who feel the commanding power of the name 'Universalist' and realize that it is a poor Universalism that prays for a universality on the other side of death which they distrust and avoid on this side." He was against "those whose universality is rimmed by some feeble creedlet, consisting of three somewhat ambiguous phrases."[174] In the Second Congress in 1894 Jones deplored the way in which the two principal denominational structures were impeding the work of "Liberaldom," like dogs in a manger.[175] The Universalist spokesman at the Congress, Dr. James M. Pullman, allowed the cogency of criticism leveled at mainline members of his denomination, "[You] Universalists [they rightly say] have squatted on the biggest word in the English language. Now the world is beginning to want that word, and you Universalists must either improve the property or move off the premises."[176]

With support from such Universalists as James Pullman, the Congress inspired the formation of what could be called locally a United Liberal Church or a People's Church.[177] It was in this same year, 1894, at Saratoga, New York, that the Unitarian denomination, under the radical influence of their Western Conference, substantially altered the basis of the National Conference, by eliminating in the Unitarian constitution article ix on "allegiance to the gospel of Jesus Christ" and by substituting for the original preamble with its references to "the disciples of the Lord Jesus Christ" and for the article on "Christian churches of the Unitarian faith" a new nonbinding reference to "the religion of Jesus" and his summary of "practical religion." Soon after the Saratoga Conference one of the editors of *The Non-Sectarian* said, "The Universalist Church is now just about where the Unitarian Church was thirty years ago. Let us hope that its progress toward union and liberty will be more rapid."[178] It was thus at the very time that the Unitarians were professedly ceasing to be Christians denominationally that they began to make overtures to the Universalists, who for their part in the language of one of their most conservative Christian spokesmen (Sweetser) were at this juncture most concerned about an "all-togetherness" in their "forward movement."

Opposition to close association with Unitarians had been vigorously expressed already in 1893 by Quillen Shinn, national missionary of the Young People's Christian Union (founded in 1889, with its motto, "For Christ and the Church"). He had declared in reference to the World Relief motif of the Western liberals,

So, I am bold to say, that so long as a sister church rests its faith on natural religion, ignoring a revealed religion, we cannot unite with that church, and it will impair our usefulness exceedingly to be associated with it in any way that will give the impression that we are one and the same. When we cease to regard Christ as authority, or the fundamental truth he revealed, then we step down as a Church off the bed-rock of spiritual faith and begin to drift into the great Universal, and the alluring Universals, which seem so fascinating to many good people who delight in calling themselves "liberals." A circumference is a good thing; a center is absolutely necessary. I am a member of the Universalist Church, not of the church Universal. One defines; the other soars into the nebulous infinitudes and fades into celestial nothingness.[179]

At the General Convention in Meriden, Connecticut, in 1895, a quarter of a century after the Centennial, the resolutions committee introduced a motion calling for Universalist–Unitarian cooperation, but the motion was tabled.[180] Yet, the forces for liberal theological change in the denomination thought that they had at least overcome the credal strictures of Winchester and Gloucester in getting passed the following substitute for the Winchester Confession in a move comparable to the change in the preamble of the Unitarian constitution at Saratoga the year before:

> We [Universalists] believe in the universal Fatherhood of God, and in the universal Brotherhood of Man. We believe that God, who hath spoken through all His holy prophets since the world began, hath spoken to us by His son Jesus Christ, our Example and Saviour. We believe that Salvation consists in spiritual oneness with God, who, through Christ, will finally gather in one the whole family of mankind.[181]

The Meriden affirmation, which constitutionally required confirmation from the subsequent convention, was turned down emphatically (with one dissenting vote!) in the next (now biennial) General Convention in Chicago in 1897.

Then two years later, the Unitarians at their May Meetings in Boston, in 1899, resolved that "in the interests of pure Christianity," the two denominations should formally move toward closer relationships.[182] There was representative reaction to this strong overture from Isaac Morgan Atwood and Edwin Chapin Sweetser, who were respectively skeptical and caustic, and from Frederic W. Perkins and Willard C. Selleck, who were favorable.

Commenting on the overture jocularly, the first general superintendent of the General Convention, Isaac M. Atwood, declared in 1899:

> The recurrence of the wooing, which has broken out at intervals for many years, between the Universalists and the Unitarians, evinces a smouldering affection somewhere under the surface. This time it is

the American Unitarian Association, a rather venerable and some-what austere lover, that gets down on one knee to the Universalist dame, also past her maiden enthusiasm, but charming still. These attacks are spontaneous, not manufactured. They spring from chronic conditions. They are in the blood. There is an affinity and kinship between the wooers which all who yield themselves fully to the movings of the spirit, in either denomination, feel. It is not so ardent and irrepressible as to carry either party quite away, or make either ready to drop the family name and welcome the loss of identity. While we should not call it mere flirtation, it is rather to be classed with a bachelor's occasional and oft cooled inflammations, intermittent and hesitant, than with the passion that foretokens wedding bells.[183]

Edwin Chapin Sweetser (1847–1929) of the Church of the Messiah in Philadelphia, who had long been at work to bring about a more conservative credal formulation of Universalism giving prominence to the work of the Holy Spirit,[184] argued truculently in "The Invitation of the American Unitarian Association (1899)."[185] He asserted his conviction thus: "Not until the Unitarians accept Jesus Christ as the Universalists do will it be advisable for the two bodies to adopt such a plan as the Unitarians have suggested."[186] He was certain that abandonment of the Lordship of Christ by the Unitarians nationally at Saratoga in 1894 (in the conviction that "there is a bigger thing coming . . . than Christianity, and that is Universal religion") had actually denoted the decadence of the Unitarian body, which in turn had emboldened them to seek an infusion of fresh vitality from the Universalists. Holding it to be "rather a philosophy or a cult, than a Christian religion . . . , an ethical culture society," Sweetser also bitterly accused the Unitarian denomination as from the beginning living "largely at the expense of other denominations, whose churches it has captured" and as "apparently regarding our churches as its legitimate prey." He was indignant that the very denomination that had invited the Universalists to join in the common cause of "pure Christianity" had the very year before officially reported that there were only five churches in the South devoted to "the gospel of liberal Christianity," perversely overlooking in characteristic haughtiness the 104 Universalist churches in those very states.[187]

As his denomination approached the General Convention in Buffalo in 1901, Sweetser went further in his bitter critique and warning "Shall We Ally Ourselves with the Unitarians?"[188] remarking with Shakespeare, "And two men ride of a horse, one must ride behind."

Frederic W. Perkins, in contrast to Sweetser recognized, in "The Unitarian Overture to the Universalist Church,"[189] "the promptings of genuine Christian catholicity" noting that "along the lines of their distinctive initial impulses the two Churches have arrived at substantially a common ground." Holding that "the Free Religious Association is an example of arrested development" in contrast to the now much more inclusive Unitarian body, and remarking that, too, "[t]he Universalist Church has learned spiritual catholicity," he asserted "the two Churches need each other in a common work."[190]

Willard C. Selleck in "What is the Difference between Universalism and Unitarianism?"[191] after rehearsing the histories of the two denominations, noted that there had been a convergence in respect to class, scholarship, theology—the Universalists having become Unitarian and the Unitarians Universalist. He then went on to note still remaining differences in accent in the concluding year of the nineteenth century. On individualism: "the Unitarian Church is like a pile of sand and the Universalist . . . a lump of clay." On religious modality and mood: "The theological interest is still stronger among Universalists than among Unitarians. . . . [and there is] a little more spiritual enthusiasm among Universalists." He noted also the lingering interest in Christology among Universalists but concluded, although he was positive to the Unitarian overture: "Thus it appears that the radical Universalists and the conservative Unitarians stand side by side; while the conservative Universalists and the radical Unitarians are pretty far apart in their thought and tendencies."

In the meantime, the effort to liberalize the Universalist Profession of Faith at the General Convention in Meriden in 1895, but reversed at Chicago in 1897, was revived under the leadership of George T. Knight of Tufts at general convention in the Boston Profession or the Declaration of Five [supplementary] Principles in 1899.[192] The most liberal leadership in the denomination at this juncture was represented by Orello Cone (1835–1905), professor of Bible at St. Lawrence (1865) and president of Buchtel College in Akron

(1880). In 1889 he had edited *Essays Doctrinal and Practical by Fifteen Clergymen,* embodying the liberal, scriptural, and theological thought in the denomination. And then in 1900 he published *Evolution and Theology and Other Essays.* This effort represented the full tide in favor of evolution that had begun soon after 1860.[193] The Boston Profession of Five Principles, while retaining the Winchester Profession in three articles, in effect revised them in such a fashion that the denomination dropped the death and glory theory which, with Murray, had presupposed the "Calvinist" doctrine of immutable predestination (made, however, applicable to all men as elect) and, instead, acknowledged, but in greatly attenuated form, the certainty of just retribution for sins in the hereafter (principle 4), while avowing a final harmony of all souls with God (principle 5).[194]

With the symptomatic Boston Declaration of Principles in 1899, even then felt to be out of date by the younger leadership, and despite vigorous and angry opposition to mingling with Unitarians from such Universalist conservatives as Dr. Sweetser, a joint committee of the two perhaps inevitably confluent denominations came into being and worked at its assignment from 1900 to about 1907. Gradually, however, the expectations of union cooled. Various kinds of fraternal cooperation were all that could be looked forward to for awhile.

In one ministerial household, we see the new mood and modality in microcosm, in that of the Universalist Reverend Florence Kollock Crooker and of the Unitarian Reverend Dr. Joseph Henry Crooker, originally a Baptist minister. She had been graduated from St. Lawrence in 1875, and he much later received his STD (1900). Before their marriage in 1896, which was for him a second marriage, Florence Kollock had served pastorates in Chicago, Pasadena, and St. Paul. His pastorates were successively in Madison, Helena, Ann Arbor, and Boston; and for ten years he was president of the Unitarian temperance society. The couple, and particularly Dr. Crooker, are being introduced at this point because they successfully maintained their separate denominational ministries after marriage and he for his part wrote three books on the Church: one for his own denomination, *The Unitarian Church: Its History and Characteristics: A Statement* (with a foreword by Samuel A. Eliot)[195] and two for his wife's denomination and publishing house, *The*

Church of Today: A Plea (1908) and *The Church of Tomorrow* (1911).[196] In the latter, in sustained allusion to the One Holy Catholic Apostolic Church, recognizing holiness in helpfulness, catholicity in hospitality, apostolicity in the willingness to "labor, suffer, and conquer for God and humanity," Crooker in reference to the oneness declared (in 1911):

> [T]he Church of Tomorrow will not be of uniform doctrine or of identical organization. There will be unity of spirit, but not uniformity of creed or rite or polity. There will be variety, but not intolerance. There will be cooperation for holiness, but not conformity of theological opinion. There will be identity of ethical enthusiasm but diversities of administrations. The truth is that different denominations, as a rule, represent different temperaments, different intellectual equipment and different social conditions. . . . In the spiritual Commonwealth that is coming there will be glad recognition of the fact that all religious bodies share in the essentials of a common Christianity.[197]

At the General Convention in 1909 at Detroit a memorial from the Missouri Convention had been introduced on eventual organic union with the Unitarians and appropriate modalities. To this and a constitutional amendment allowing for joint ministerial fellowship with Unitarians (and others) Sweetser made violent objection. The General Convention concluded "that organic union be left to make its own way as the divine spirit of truth and Christian brotherhood may move our hearts."[198] And we see that in the hearts of Reverends Joseph and Florence Crooker it was possible to keep the two denominations lovingly distinct. The World War interrupted any further efforts to find a *modus vivendi* with the Unitarians, and at the sesquicentennial at Gloucester in 1920, a former member of the Universalist–Unitarian joint committee was still thinking of the denominations as quite distinct streams. An exponent of Christian Universalism, Dr. John Coleman Adams (1849–1922) of Hartford, now identified Liberalism as America's Broad Church movement, likening it to the Mississippi with two major tributaries, the Missouri and the Ohio, respectively, the Universalists and the Unitarians.[199] But he recognized lesser tributaries of Liberalism, the Hicksite

Quakers and Methodists, "a liberalizing element." John Coleman Adams, son of the Reverend John Greenleaf Adams (who had attended the Centennial and was author of *Fifty Notable Years,* 1882)[200] retained clearly, even after the upheaval of World War I, the vision of the distinctive mission of Christian Universalism.[201] And this was in part because many Universalists felt closer to the Congregationalists than to the Unitarians.

Relations With Congregationalists, 1913–1927

Apparently the first introduction of a possible Universalist–Congregationalist entente was at the General Convention in Chicago in 1913 when Dr. John Coleman Adams and Dr. L. B. Fisher formulated a greeting to the Congregationalists at their national conference in Kansas City, expressing, among other fraternal sentiments, "the hope that the coming years may draw both bodies of Christians into a closer unity of the spirit in the service of Jesus Christ."[202]

In 1916 Dr. Lee McCollester, moderator of the Convention (1915–1917), declared,

> We must overcome our ignorance of each other by entire frankness in speech and dealing, and command mutual respect and a recognition of the difficulties in the way: prejudices and traditions which may be outgrown, adjustment of funds, and laws of fellowship. We need especially the mixing of our people in local parishes and a working union with liberal Congregationalists as well as Unitarians.[203]

The war interrupted further rapprochement; but it is notable that as the denomination emerged from that upheaval (sobered in its inherent optimism) to celebrate its sesquicentennial in Gloucester in 1920, that among the many speakers, the Congregationalist spokesman at the interdenominational meeting could, in the euphoria of the occasion, refer to the body he represented and to the two others represented on the platform as, respectively, "Universalist Puritans," "Congregationalist Puritans," and "Unitarian Puritans."[204] The Congregationalist speaking was Dr. William E. Barton, who enhanced his credentials by observing that he had just completed the first draft of his book on, and edition of, the papers of Clara Barton, who had expressly chosen him for her funeral service; and it was with considerable historical and theological specificity that as a rather conservative Trinitarian predestinarian he could still demonstrate that the three essentially New England denominations had very much in common.

The initiative for actual merger with the Congregationalists arose in the Maine Convention in 1925.[205] The General Convention in Syracuse in 1925 under the moderatorship of John Murray Atwood, dean of the Theological School at St. Lawrence (1914–1951), received from both the Unitarians and the Congregationalists[206] overtures for cooperation. A committee worked from 1925 to 1927 on a joint Universalist–Congregationalist statement. The finished proposal was accepted at the General Convention in Hartford in 1927 as providing closer fellowship with Congregationalist churches, but the Convention insisted that the approval of the joint statement did not commit Universalists to "organic union."[207] Although there were to be subsequent interdenominational meetings, the proposal for merely increased fellowship was tabled by the Congregationalists because of the inhibiting restraints imposed by the Universalists at Hartford.[208]

Although later the denomination would seek membership in the Federal Council of Churches, the chief proponent of this doubled effort (1944; 1946), Dr. Robert Cummins, general superintendent (1938–1953), is probably closer to the facts when he argues that the leadership of the denomination, if not the rank-and-file, were primarily attracted to the council by the opportunity afforded for enlarged social action than by Christian ecumenism. He said before the General Convention in New York in 1943:

> Universalism cannot be limited either to Protestantism or to Christianity, not without denying its very name. Ours is a world fellowship, not just a Christian sect. For so long as Universalism *is* universalism and not partialism, the fellowship bearing its name must succeed in making it unmistakably clear that *all* are welcome: theist and humanist, unitarian and trinitarian, colored and color-less. A circumscribed Universalism is unthinkable.[209]

In any case the sustained reserve of the Universalists as to joining either the Unitarians (1890–1917) or the Congregationalists (1913–

1927) must be understood as explicitly or latently a consequence of the deep sense nurtured in the hearts of most Universalists throughout almost two centuries of their history that they had a unique mission as a church, and this is reflected in the extraordinary formulations of their concept of universal salvation and of the Universalist Church. Over against "partialism" they embraced together an ever-widening meaning of Universalism for members of the denomination. We turn therefore to some of their concurrent formulations of Universalism as a world religion.

From Universal Christianity to Universal Religion, 1893–1946

In the period from the World's Parliament of Religions to the end of the Second World War, the minor strand among the ecclesiologies in the Centennial year of 1870, associated then eccentrically with Adin Ballou and exceptionally with Herman Bisbee, would become the dominant strand in the denomination, either latently, inadvertently, or quite programmatically.

We have already overheard C. Ellwood Nash in 1899[210] anticipate the evolution of Universalism into "the universal religion" and we have just heard Robert Cummins, a half-century later, on the very eve of the effort to join the Federal Council of Churches, repudiate every "partialism," and his assertion that "A circumscribed Universalism is unthinkable."[211]

One of the leading theologians of Universalism in his period was James Minton Pullman (d. 1903), brother of the Reverend Royal H. and the paternalistic Chicago industrialist George Mortimer Pullman (d. 1897), founder of the Pullman Palace Car Company. On the occasion of the centennial of the Winchester Profession of Faith, James Pullman may be overheard in 1903 giving expression to the transition from an older to a new conception of Universalism on the road to world religion:

> Universalism as a faith is just universalized Christianity, a strict development of Christianity out of its special into its universal form—the central teaching of Jesus taken out from under provincial and encumbering accretions and turned to a universal faith.[212]

Mindful no doubt of his famous industrialist brother, Pullman, referring to the earth "as God's workshop" and to the "moral product" of the globe as character, propounded, as an optimistic evolutionist in 1903, a rather extraordinary cosmic Universalism, more confident than that even of the much later Teilhard de Chardin:

> The order of nature in which we live is, first of all, a mind factory—a machine for transmitting matter into mind by means both of the brute and human organisms. And we export every year, through what we call death, about thirty-five million minds, in germ and in all stages of development, to the other worlds of the universe. Our works and ways thus run out into the cosmos and we are cooperating with the whole.[213]

Clarence Russell Skinner (1881–1949) was, of course, a major exponent of Universalism as the Universal Church and Universal Religion. Son of the editor of the *Brooklyn Eagle*, Charles Montgomery Skinner, he gave a paper at the sesquicentennial in Gloucester in 1920 under the general symposium heading: "The Universalism of the Future."[214] He had but recently written "Some Principles of the Future Religion."[215] Clarence Skinner, influential dean of Crane Theological School at Tufts (1933–1945), was cofounder and original theorist of Community Church in Boston. Originally called to Tufts from his church and forum in Lowell, Massachusetts, to become in 1914 professor of Applied Christianity, he carried into the period between World War I and II impulses that may well have stemmed from as far back as the published sermon of his grandfather, the Reverend Charles Augustus Skinner of Somerville, Massachusetts, in 1890, "Applied Universalism."[216] On the nature of the Church and Universalism, Clarence Skinner expressed himself notably in a series of lectures given on the occasion of the founding of the Community Church in Boston in the sesquicentennial year 1920, entitled "The Church as a Universal Community"[217] and in *A Religion for Greatness* (1945). For him Universalism was a radical religion, breaking programmatically from the past, concerned with both unities and universals, manifested or to be manifested in economic, social, political, racial, and scientific Universalism.

Dr. Tracy Pullman (b. 1904), grandson of the already cited Dr. James M. and grandnephew of the founder of the Pullman

Company, when minister in Detroit (1940–1968), made one of the most explicit statements in mainline Universalism as to its being the forerunner of the world religion. In a printed sermon, *A Religion Greater than Christianity* (Detroit, 1946), he declared, summing up his vision:

> Here, then is a suggested pattern of the new religion. It is greater than Christianity because it is an evolutionary religion, because it is universal rather than partial, because it is one with the spirit of science and is primarily interested in bringing out that which is God-like in man.

The Humiliati (from 1945 on), a Tufts-based fellowship inspired by the ideals of Dean Skinner, as also clearly articulated by the Tufts divinity alumnus Tracy Pullman (1926), expressed their conviction about universal religion in their symbol of an off-center cross. They saw in the Community Church of Boston one embodiment of the ideal of religion embracing the interests of all classes of society and all temperaments and aptitudes of men. They saw in that church and their fellowship an authentic continuation not only of the ideal of the "New Civilization" of Adin Ballou,[218] but also of the basic principle of John Murray himself, who had postulated Christ's death as intended for the salvation of all mankind whether Christ's name was known or unknown, whether expressly acknowledged or unheeded. The Humiliati were explicit about this continuity in their mimeographed leaflet series, *Theologically Speaking*: "Universalism is in very truth the religion for survival. . . . This 'New' Universalism is not new at all. It is firmly rooted in the thinking of our father in the faith, Hosea Ballou."[219] In answer to the question as to why the cross was not put in the center, the Humiliati answered: "Because Christianity is not central or even necessary to Universalism. . . . The important feature of the symbol is the circle and not the cross." Contemplating this off-center cross, these Humiliati betokened by the symbol their conviction that Universalism is the important emphasis of religion for today; that Universalism is found in the highest development of all the world religions; that the universals transcend the partialisms of every religious faith, including Christianity; that Christianity has been an important step for us in reaching Universalism; that Universalism is a higher development than traditional Christianity.[220]

The World Religion thrust in Universalism found balanced expression in two Greater Boston events in 1949. In that year Clinton Lee Scott of Tufts published his *Religion Can Make Sense,* a representative compendium of Universalist theology for the post–World War II period, with chapter xix on "What a Church Is" and chapter xxxv, "Are Americans a Chosen People?" to which he gave a universalist answer. Also in 1949 Unitarian-trained Kenneth Patton (b. 1911) became controversial minister of the programmatic effort to recover in the Charles Street Meeting House a fresh base for Universalism in Boston, just 140 years after the voice of John Murray was silenced by sickness. Patton published a cascade of leaflets and volumes on art, experimental liturgy, and ethics—most representatively *A Religion for One World: Art and Symbols for a Universal Religion* (1964). Espousing a unitive, naturalistic-mystical-humanistic World Religion, he was challenged by the more conservative members of the local association; and denominational fellowship with him became a touchstone of a truly impartialist Universalism.

CONCLUSION

When I was asked to prepare a bicentennial essay with special attention to the impact of Universalism on American society, I was not then so fully aware of what I now surmise, having made my soundings in that extraordinary deep pool of sources at the Universalist Historical Library at Tufts! American Universalism is a much more complex movement than American Unitarianism. The devolution of the doctrine of the Trinity with attendant philanthropic and eventually sociocritical concerns is much easier to follow in the surviving documentation and to rehearse in a standard denominational history than the universalization of Christianity with attendant philanthropic concerns *interconnected* at one and the same time and often in the same person (a) with America the redeemer nation of manifest global destiny, (b) with the socio-political model of the ancient Church nurtured in, but critical of, the Roman imperial *oikoumene,* and (c) with the restoration of that primitive ideal both in organized religion and in society at large in an orientation that has been at times not only futurist but eschatologically millennialist. Moreover, this universalizing Christianity, which moved from the transcendence alike of Protestantism and Catholicism as "partialist" to a self-estimate of Universalism as either *the* world religion itself or at least its most persuasive harbinger, was also from the beginning understood as part of a cosmic drama.

Both John Murray and Elhanan Winchester could confidently foresee the restoration of humanity to holiness and happiness because of the work of Christ, head of the race, understood by them as at once fully man and fully God. Their high Christology in the context of the unchallenged doctrine of the Trinity made it possible, indeed, for Murray to assert that Christ as the Last Adam had once for all assumed the full penal burden of the sin of the first Adam and all his descendents, opening to all mankind the gates of heaven. Yet as dependent as Murrayan Universalism was on this high Christology joined to an unimpaired Triadology, it was precisely a Universalist Father, Hosea Ballou, who as early as 1805, *first* expounded unitarianism in a programmatic repudiation of the Calvinist theory of the atonement. But in undoing Calvin and Anselm, Ballou also undid Murray and unwittingly obliged the followers of Murray and Winchester arduously to relocate the theological foundations of their Universalist hope in a regionally part-Unitarian context.

It has been somewhat important, in this bicentennial essay, to insist on New England (with New York) as the engendering and influential region in Universalist history in order to account for the early acceptance of Ballou's unitarianism, so prejudicial in the end to Murray's universalism. Had Murray and Winchester proclaimed their Universalist Restorationism in regions largely unaffected by the Unitarian challenge from *within* prestigious established churches (in Massachusetts, Maine, and New Hampshire) and in the oldest college of that region, their Universalism might have evolved more like the Campbellite Restorationism of the Disciples of Christ (Christians). To be sure Alexander Campbell *(Declaration and Address,* 1809) was seeking a restoration of the norms of the primitive church in order to get away from Protestant divisiveness, and his restorationism was accordingly more "ecumenically" than eschatologically Universalist, although he was also, like the early Universalists, millennialist. Moreover, the Campbellites based their faith and polity primarily on the New Testament *(A Restoration of the Ancient Order of Things,* 1825) rather than equally on the whole Bible, as with Murray and Winchester. Given therefore the New England genesis of Universalism, with emerging denominational headquarters in the same city with both Unitarians and

Congregationalists, it is almost as important for Universalist history as for that of the two other Boston-centered denominations that proto-Unitarianism prevailed academically in 1805 in the appointment of Henry Ware, Sr., as Hollis Professor at Harvard in the same year as Ballou's *Atonement;* that Unitarianism became juridically visible in the Massachusetts–Maine establishments in the Dedham Decision of 1820 (allowing for the distinction throughout the area between a First Parish with meetinghouse and a First Church with communion plate and new meetinghouse to be built); and that Unitarianism became denominationally visible with the formation of the Association in 1825. Although the Universalist Ballou had boldly formulated unitarianism in northern Vermont, Universalists everywhere, especially in New England, were drawn to it. Yet they must also have long begrudged the establishmentarian Unitarians themselves for their preeminence in proclaiming precisely as their central tenet the very doctrine which, while it consolidated their own denomination and clearly differentiated it from others, would, like a two-edged sword, theologically disrupt Universalists because it cut into Murray's rather high, christologically based Universalism and tended also to undercut the attempt of Hosea Ballou, 2d, to reclaim for the denomination the prestigious patristic Universalism of Origen and the rest (likewise highly christological and triadological). The fact, moreover, that the intellectual development of Universalism in its engendering region took place where establishmentarian Unitarians dominated the terrain (disestablishment took place in Massachusetts as late as 1833) meant also the inhibition of the incipient Universalist thrust toward scriptural-patristic (ecclesiological) restoration (analogous to that in the Campbellite movement of the Disciples of Christ) of both Hosea Ballou, 2d, and Adin Ballou. Therewith began to fade also any christocentric eschatogical Universalism. By the mid-twentieth century, there were only three denominational alternatives left: representation as one more Protestant denomination regathered in the fold with others in the Council of Churches, nationalist democratic faith, or the global humanism of world religion.

The first option was indeed tried, unsuccessfully, in the 1940s. Despite the Americanist motif from Winchester through Washburn, the denomination had had too much experience of being outside the mainstream to be willing to acquiesce in any uncritical Christian nationalism. Thus in the end it chose after nearly two centuries to merge with the very denomination whose name signaled the very doctrine by which Murray's christocentric Universalism had been undone from within and from without. But it merged at a time when a large contingent in the Unitarian and a substantial contingent in the Universalist denomination had become humanist. And an important assessment needs therefore yet to be made as to whether Universalist humanism still carries in it significant impulses from Murray, Winchester, and the three Ballous.

With John Murray and in the course of two hundred years' development, Universalism has perceived its mission as the affirmation of the restoration of all creation in ultimate harmony; and with Murray himself and many another this has meant the created order in general, as well as humanity. We may recall here in this line of thought the words of Quillen Shinn in 1900: "Neither a single atom nor a single soul can get beyond the reach of this Almighty force of love so that it is unable to draw back. . . . We believe no such catastrophe [as eternal discord] can happen. Nature means victory."[1]

The Boston wit, brother-in-law of Longfellow, who coined the most enduring epigram on Universalists and Unitarians, the latter confident in man's goodness and the former in the goodness of the ultimate force behind the creation of both nature and our human condition,[2] is still a pointer to what the Universalist component in the merged denomination can mean for us of a generation rocked by ecological crises and more fearful of a cosmic catastrophe than hopeful of a benign millennium, namely, the formative Universalist confidence that there is a powerful and benign force at work within us, about us, at the interior of being and above it, that sustains our hope. On the two-hundredth anniversary of the landing of humane and all-embracing John Murray at Good Luck on the Atlantic coast, we can with him and in the encouraging company of generations of valiant and extraordinarily happy, highly motivated people, called Universalists, count on more than "good luck" for the century ahead, not wholly because of the inherent and unambiguous goodness of men—on this we have been sobered and perhaps even alarmed—

but because of the sustaining powers in the cosmos, which, as Universalists so early perceived, is at once our celestial and our earthly home.

May all these our forebears or jointly adopted spiritual ancestors help us in new ways, as Shinn said of one of the Universalist female penologists, to reach "the mother nature in the most refractory women" and to perceive the divine paternity in all men, and all this because we have reglimpsed the vision of John Murray, as he once in England knelt and prayed directly to "dear parent earth,"[3] deeply sensible of the ultimate benevolence not only of his stern father and his well-to-do adoptive father but also of the Almighty, the ultimate *mysterium tremendum et fascinosum*, whose awesome compassion will not let a single soul or atom get beyond the reach of his purposeful love.

NOTES

Introduction

1. The Universalist Centennial held in Gloucester, Massachusetts, September 20th, 21st, and 22nd, 1870. Universalist Church of America, *Proceedings at the Universalist Centennial Held in Gloucester, Massachusetts, September 20th, 21st, and 22nd, 1870* (Boston: Universalist Publishing House, 1870, p. 105A.

2. Clinton Lee Scott gives prominence to the Middle Colonies and the German sectarian restorationist impulses by making of them the first chapter in his *The Universalist Church of America* (Boston: Universalist Historical Society, 1957), but he, too, acknowledges that New England was the effectual cradle of the denomination. The principal links between German sectarian universalism and the American Universalism of Elhanan Winchester are as follows: Winchester read the *Everlasting Gospel* [cf. Rev. 14:8] by "Paul Siegvolck" (Georg Klein-Nikolai), published in English by Christopher Saur (born in the Pietist center of Wittgenstein) in Germantown in 1753 (which Winchester reedited in 1792); he read *Universal Restitution: A Scripture Doctrine* (London, 1761), and *Vindicated* (1773) by the Rev. Sir James Stonehouse; and he made the acquaintance of the Huguenot universalist physician and near martyr Dr. Georges de Benneville (1703–1793), whose *Life and Trance* he edited in 1791. On the

---

Many of the endnotes refer to the Universalist Historical Library at Tufts University. Since this book's original publication, the collection has been transferred and is now part of the Universalist Special Collections at Andover-Harvard Theological Library.

85

steps by which Winchester accepted and proclaimed "Siegvolck's" views, see most recently and vividly Charles White McGehee, "Elhanan Winchester: A Decision for Universal Restoration," *Journal of the Universalist Historical Society, I* (1959), pp. 43–58. Albert D. Bell, *The Life and Times of George de Benneville* (Boston: Universalist Church of America, 1953) was convinced that Germanic Pietism with universalist implications was a major component in the spread of organized Universalism in America. And David A. Johnson in "George de Benneville and the Heritage of the Radical Reformation," *Journal of the Universalist Historical Society, VIII* (1969–70), pp. 25–43, has most effectively assembled the data that demonstrate the confluence of several impulses from the Radical Reformation and later German Pietism into the religious culture, on which Universalism in Pennsylvania most certainly drew at various stages in the evolution of the denomination. There is furthermore no doubt but that the feeling for the transcendent, the otherworldly, for dreams, visions, and parapsychological phenomena; sometimes speculative interest in the androgynous Adam and in the heavenly Sophia; and also concern for group discipline, so conspicuous in sectarianism, remained components in Universalism from Murray and especially Winchester well into all the last third of the nineteenth century. See, for example, on spiritualism, below, at n. 106, ch. 2, etc. Geoffrey Rowell of New College, Oxford, was unaware of the studies of Scott, McGehee, Bell, and Johnson aforementioned, in his otherwise very fully documented "The Origins and History of Universalist Societies in Britain [esp. London, Scotland, and Wales], 1750–1850," *Journal of Ecclesiastical History, XXII* (Jan. 1971), pp. 35–56.

Using Walter Wilson, *The History and Antiquities of the Dissenting Churches and Meeting Houses of London, Westminster, and Southwark,* 4 vols. (London, 1808–10) and Nils Thun, *The Behmenists* [English followers of Jakob Böhme, who was not himself a universalist] *and Philadelphians* (1948), Rowell not only adds much regional and biographical specificity to the still-obscure mosaic of British universalism in general but also provides new data and a fresh context for the London career of Winchester, pp. 39–42, and for Murray and both James and John Relly, pp. 45–49.

3. The first convention beyond this engendering region was at Akron, Ohio, in 1843. Then followed Baltimore in 1844; Cincinnati in 1849; Columbus in 1853; Chicago in 1857; Galesburg, Illinois, in 1866; and Baltimore again in 1867. Of the 133 General Conventions between 1793 and 1960, only forty or less than one-third were held outside the regions of New England and New York.

4. The bon mot goes back to Thomas Gold Appleton (1812–1884), brother-

in-law of Henry Wadsworth Longfellow.

That Universalists were back-country in their New England origin should not be converted into a cliché or denominational myth. Universalism entered the larger cities in due course and was surely no more suspicious of the vicious effects of the cities than the evangelicals. When the congregational standing order in Massachusetts, Maine, and New Hampshire went in part Unitarian in 1820/25, many small-town churches were caught up into the newly emergent association/denomination.

5. "Address of Rev. E. E. Hale," *Proceedings,* op. cit. n. 1, p. 69B.

6. July 18, 1870.

7. The French Emperor and the army capitulated after the Battle of Sedan, September 1, 1870.

8. There had been a cable laid in 1858 but it broke. In 1886 a new and abiding cable was laid.

9. The Union Pacific joined, with a golden spike, the Central Pacific (building eastward) at Promontory, Utah, May 10, 1869.

10. *Proceedings,* op. cit. n. 1, p. 69A.

11. We catch their suspicion as of the previous decade in the reminiscence of the Reverend Erasmus Manford of St. Louis toward the Universalists struggling in St. Louis, circa 1861:

    I hear of the love of Unitarians for us, but have never seen much evidence of their affection. They doubtless would like to have Unitarians and Universalists unite, but it must be like the marriage of man and woman, according to Blackstone—the twain one, and that one, Unitarian. Erasmus Manford, *Twenty-five Years in the West,* 3rd ed. (Chicago: H. B. Manford, 1885), p. 304.

12. *Proceedings,* op. cit. n. 1, p. 42. It might be further remarked that the cornerstone of the church in Nantucket (1325) contained a lock of Murray's hair. Alan Seaburg, "Universalism in Nantucket," *Historic Nantucket, XIV* (July 1966), pp. 5–9.

13. Ibid., p. 55. The orator was Mrs. Mary Livermore.

14. John Murray, *The Life of Rev. John Murray,* centennial ed. (Boston: Munroe and Francis, 1870).

15. A new critical edition is a desideratum partly because of the important references to, and quotation of, contemporary divines whose works have been subsequently edited, for example to John Wesley in his home, p. 111; to George Whitfield, whom he preferred, pp. 96, 117; to Tennant, with whom he had a theological altercation, pp. 233f.; and to Samuel Hopkins, with whom he held theological conversation in the same stage coach into Newport, p. 245; and partly because of extraordinary numbers of inti-

mate details shared by the autobiographer of special interest to psychological interpreters of religion. (On this last, see what is said at n. 24, ch. 2.) For Mrs. Murray, see Vena B. Field, *Constantia: A Study of the Life and Work of Judith Sargent Murray, 1751–1820,* University of Maine Studies, 2nd series, no. 17 (Orono, ME: University Press, 1931).

16. *Life of Rev. John Murray*, op. cit. n. 14, p. 13.

17. *Proceedings*, op. cit. n. 1, p. 105B.

18. Ibid., pp. 76–78, 109B.

19. Exodus 28:2 reads, "[T]hou shalt make holy garments for Aaron." Interpreting Jesus Christ as the high priest, Murray declared that he clothed himself with mankind making human nature holy. John Murray, *Letters and Sketches of Sermons,* vol. 3 (Boston: J. Belcher, 1813), p. 11.

20. The best exposition and criticism of Murray's imperfectly worded distinction between universal redemption (God's intention) and salvation (limited human awareness of this nevertheless universal blessing) is probably that of Hosea Ballou, 2d, "Dogmatic and Religious History of Universalism in America," *Universalist Quarterly,* V (January 1848), pp. 79–103; substantially excerpted and helpfully supplemented by Richard Eddy, *Universalism in America,* vol. 1 (Boston: Universalist Publishing House, 1886), pp. 151–163.

The doctrine of Christ's headship of humanity in Murray and before him in Relly has marked affinities with that in the later Scottish theologians, Thomas Erskine, John McLeod Campbell, and Edward Irving (in London the father of the Irvingites or Plymouth Brethren). The English Unitarian turned Anglican, Frederick Denison Maurice, in part stimulated by these divines, also made Christ's headship of humanity central to his whole system. Common to all these Britishers was the same conviction expressed by Murray, namely, that faith or salvation consisted in discerning what had always been, as when lifting mist reveals the contours of the mountains and valleys. Maurice in *The Life of Frederick Denison Maurice, Chiefly Told in His Own Letters,* edited by his son Frederick Maurice, 2 vols. (London: Charles Scribner's Sons, 1884), vol. 1, p. 208, and vol. 2, pp. 15–20, insisted that he was never a Universalist; but the context of his remarks makes it evident that he referred especially to patristic (Origenistic) universalism; for Maurice emphatically said much the same as Murray, namely, that Jesus simply made clear what the Father had always willed for humanity. Further investigation may establish genetic connections in addition to these analogues and bring out further that the nonevangelical broadchurchmanship of Unitarian/Anglican Maurice is one British counterpart of American Universalism, which, to be sure, under American Unitarian influence, in part, lost its original Logos–Adam Christology. Cf. "Origins," op. cit. n. 2, pp. 53f. on Thomas Erskine in the universalist context.

With reference to Arminianism in contrast to "Calvinism" in the main text above and elsewhere in the book, a supplementary word of clarification is useful. New England Calvinism (Puritanism) yielded in part to Arminianism in the second half of the eighteenth century, and this in turn led to Unitarianism. Among the Arminians was the anti-revivalist Charles Chauncy (d. 1787) of First Church, Boston. Unrepresentatively, he became himself an exponent of Arminian universalism (cf. *Proceedings*, op. cit. n. 1). The authoritative study here is that of Conrad Wright, "Arminianism in Massachusetts, 1735–1780," Harvard doctoral dissertation, Cambridge, 1943, published as *The Beginnings of Unitarianism in America* (Boston: Starr King Press, 1955). Therein Wright refers to Murray's "Calvinistic universalism," pp. 189–192, and sees that only on leaving Murray's position did Massachusetts Universalists shift "to Arminian grounds," p. 189, n.10. Wright's characterization is valid in the context of the meaning of Arminianism in Massachusetts at the time of Murray's organization of the Universalist church in Gloucester in 1779. There are, however, several major and quite distinguishable versions of Arminianism (as indeed there are of Calvinism): that of Jacob Arminius (d. 1609) himself; that of his Dutch followers, the Remonstrants; that of the party of Archbishop William Laud (d. 1645), High Church Anglicanism, as pilloried by the Puritans; that of John Wesley (d. 1791), Methodist Arminianism; and that of congregationalist Massachusetts. Whereas the seventeenth-century debate within the Reformed tradition between faithful Calvinists and revisionist Arminians centered on the questions of free will and the scope of the divine decrees of predestination and reprobation, in the eighteenth-century debate in Massachusetts Arminianism was identified not only with the original issues but now also with a shifting of effectual election from the divine decrees to the moral life, a lowering of Christology, and a dissolution of the doctrine of the solidarity of mankind in the sin of Adam. That sin was personal, like knowledge, rather than corporate and derivative became a distinctive feature of Massachusetts Arminianism, in part because of the wide circulation of the works of the English Nonconformist and Hebraist, John Taylor of Norwich (d. 1701), especially his Scripture Doctrine of Original Sin (J. Wilson, 1740); Beginnings, op. cit. n. 20, ch. 3. Murray, unlike Chauncy, retained the orthodox Christian (hence also Calvinist, but also classical Arminian) view of the solidarity of mankind in the sin of Adam and of

Christ's headship of the race as the Second Adam. Thus Murray in Massachusetts in Taylorian terms was indeed "Calvinist" because an Arminian in the Standing Order of his time would have given up the idea of the solidarity of the sin of mankind in Adam. But it should be borne in mind that for classical Calvinism Christ is the head of the elect only, whereas for classical Arminianism Christ is precisely the (intentionally redemptive) head of all mankind. New England Arminians who became expressly Unitarian (unlike exceptional Chauncy, the Arminian universalist) for some time retained the view that Christ would not effectually redeem all mankind, whereas "Calvinist"/"Arminian" Murray declared precisely that as head of the race Christ had indeed already saved all mankind. Murray and Chauncy, each universalist on his own separate ground, had comparable views on the initial Calvinist–Arminian problem of free will and faith. Hosea Ballou, in contrast, was a necessitarian or determinist like the Unitarian Joseph Priestley (d. 1804). Within the New England context the followers of Murray and Ballou came to construe their Universalism as coordinate with Calvinism and Arminianism as one of the three major conceptions of salvation. On this, see the very useful table of the contrasting positions (for Arminianism read existentially Unitarianism, Methodism, and Freewill Baptism) by the Reverend E. E. Guild, *The Universalist's Book of Reference* (Boston: Universalist Publishing House, 1853), pp. 376f. Most Universalist books on theology and church history deal only sparingly or not at all with Calvinism and Arminianism. The interrelationship in Britain and America between the two in dismantling Calvinism is deserving of further attention.

Universalist Conceptions of the Church, circa 1870

1. See *Minutes of the General Convention, 1870* (New York: J. Sutton and Co., 1871), pp. 53–95.
2. Adin Ballou called it, indeed, "Christian Sociology" in *Primitive Christianity and Its Corruptions*, vol. 3 (Lowell, MA: Thompson and Hill, 1900), p. 3.
3. The Reich, consequent upon the victory at Sedan, September 1, 1870, was not founded until January 18, 1871.
4. The troops of King Victor Emmanuel, after the departure, because of the defeat at Sedan, of the protective troops of Napoleon III in support of the Papacy, breached the walls of Rome at Porta Pia and entered papal Rome to make it the capital of the United Kingdom of Italy on September 18, 1870.

5. The Constitution of the General Convention as ratified by the Gloucester Convention in art. iii, item 3 required "*expressed assent* to the Confession of Faith"; the same also in that of the proposed parish constitution, art. iii, item 1. The Winchester formulary is variously referred to in Universalist history as Affirmation, Confession, Declaration, and Profession. *Minutes 1870*, op. cit. n. 1, pp. 62–81.

6. The last publication expressly holding to the Trinity was apparently that of a congregation in Charleston, SC, *The Evangelists' Manual: or a Guide to Trinitarian Universalists* (Charleston, SC: A. F. Cunningham, 1829).

7. Cf. this phrasing to that in the Winchester Profession of 1803, quoted below at the beginning of the section on the ordination of women.

8. Articles printed in full in Richard Eddy, *Universalism in America* (Boston: Universalist Publishing House, 1886), p. 176.

9. Cf. C. Conrad Wright, *The Liberal Christians* (Boston: Unitarian Universalist Association, 1970), p. 121 and p. 140 n. 22.

10. See below, at n. 96 in this chapter.

11. The title of Dean Clarence Skinner's last book in 1945, on his retiring from Tufts, was intended to point to Universalism as the church of the global community.

12. On Brownson's pre-Catholic ecclesiology, see George K. Malone, *The True Church: A Study in the Apologetics of Orestes Augustus Brownson* (Mundelein, IL: Saint Mary of the Lake Seminary, 1957) and also the forthcoming dissertation at the University of Virginia by William J. Gilmore, who, in his determination to provide an adequate interpretative framework for the nonrevivalistic churches in the period from 1800 to 1830, places Brownson in a setting with other Universalists like Abner Kneeland, Adin Ballou, and Edward Turner, and employs the hitherto unexploited diary kept by Brownson from his Old-Side Presbyterian phase, documenting his conversion to Universalism (1823–1825). For the whole life see Arthur Schlesinger, Jr., *Orestes A. Brownson: A Pilgrim's Progress* (Boston: Little, Brown and Co., 1939) and the projected intellectual biography by Gilmore, of which his dissertation is but a part.

There was, of course, no Catholic expression, as such, in the denomination, but the conversion of Brownson is the occasion to remark that Universalists were both repelled and fascinated by Catholicism—its global universality, its sociological inclusiveness, its "Semi-Pelagian" stress on free will and on works, and the counterpart of their own "Arminianism" in the context of the Augustinian-Reformed tradition. A study of Universalist attitudes toward Catholicism from Brownson to Brooks (below, at n. 60 in this chapter) would be instructive. See James D. Hunt, "Orestes A.

Brownson: Our Man in The Catholic Church," *The Unitarian Universalist Christian, XXV* (Nos. 3–4, 1969–70), pp. 38–42.

13. *Proceedings at the Universalist Centennial Held in Gloucester, Massachusetts, September 20th, 21st, and 22nd, 1870* (Boston: Universalist Publishing House, 1870), pp. 28–41.

14. Robert Wallace, *Antitrinitarian Biography,* 3 vols. (London: E. T. Whitfield, 1850).

15. *A History of Unitarianism,* 2 vols. (Cambridge, MA: Harvard University Press, 1945).

16. See, for example below, at n. 134 in ch. 2.

17. *Proceedings,* op. cit. n. 13, p. 40B.

18. Ibid., p. 40B.

19. Hosea Starr Ballou, *Hosea Ballou, 2nd, D.D.; First President of Tufts College: His Origin, Life, and Letters* (Boston: E. P. Guild and Co., 1896), ch. 6. For a recent interpretation, see Russell E. Miller, "Hosea Ballou 2nd: Scholar and Educator," *JUHS, I* (1959), pp. 59–79.

20. John G. Adams, *Memoir of Thomas Whittemore, D.D.* (Boston: Universalist Publishing House, 1878) shows the range of Whittemore's ministerial, political, and financial activities but does not go into the history. Whittemore published *The Early Days of Thomas Whittemore: An Autobiography Extending from a.d. 1800 to a.d. 1825* (Boston: James M. Usher, 1859).

21. These two volumes contain long excerpts from important writings and a most valuable calendared bibliography of all Universalist books and periodicals, numbering 2,278 items, from 1753 to 1888. *JUHS* should undertake to print addenda. The Widener Library copy, for example, has seventeen addenda and corrigenda.

22. It is true that rural New England, Midwestern, and then Southern Universalism had much less of this historic and scriptural–theological concern than the published writings of seaboard leaders of the denomination that are the basis of this generalization.

23. Cited by Miner in the translation of William H. Channing, *Introduction to Ethics,* including a critical survey of moral systems, 2nd ed., 2 vols. (Boston: Hilliard, Gray and Co., 1841).

24. Ernest Cassara, "The Effect of Darwinism on Universalist Belief, 1860–1900," *JUHS, 1* (1959), pp. 32–42, based intentionally on articles in *The Universalist Quarterly and General Review,* founded in 1844 by Hosea Ballou, 2d and edited after him successively by George H. Emerson (1858–1864), Thomas B. Thayer (1864–1888), and Richard Eddy (1886–1891). Cassara shows that after a momentary recoil at Darwin's *The Origin of*

Species (1859) under Emerson, *The Review* under Thayer was increasingly sympathetic.

25. The definitive Life is that of Ernest Cassara, *Hosea Ballou: The Challenge to Orthodoxy* (Boston: Universalist Historical Society, 1961).

26. *Proceedings,* op. cit. n. 13, p. 81A. Dr. Gerherdus L. Demarest was commonly quoted as saying that by 1870 Universalism had become a Church with a capital "C."

27. The title of his article in *The Universalist Quarterly and General Review, I* (Boston, 1864), pp. 103–111.

28. Ibid., p. 110; the Clarke characterization, ibid., n. 1.

29. Address in *Proceedings,* op. cit. n. 13, pp. 42–44, this passage p. 43B. On Fisk's presidency, see Louis H. Pink and Rutherford E. Delmage, eds., *Candle in the Wilderness: A Centennial History of the St. Lawrence University* (New York: Appleton-Century-Crofts, 1957), pp. 17–20.

30. *Proceedings,* op. cit. n. 13, p. 43A.

31. Address printed in *Proceedings,* op. cit. n. 13, pp. 69–72, this passage p. 70B. For more, see John Wesley Hanson, *Biography of William Henry Ryder, D.D.* (Boston: Universalist Publishing House, 1891).

32. Sumner Ellis, *Life of Edwin H. Chapin, D.D.* (Boston: Universalist Publishing House, 1883).

33. The sermon is printed in *Proceedings,* op. cit. n. 13, pp. 86–93, this passage p. 92B.

34. John Murray, *The Life of Rev. John Murray,* centennial ed. (Boston: Munroe and Francis, 1870), pp. 146 passim.

35. *Proceedings,* op. cit. n. 13, p. 90B.

36. It gives its name to a collection of sermons published posthumously as Edwin H. Chapin, *The Church of the Living God* (New York: J. Miller, 1881), pp. 9–27.

37. Translated by Francis Cunningham as *Text-Book of Ecclesiastical History,* 3 vols. (Philadelphia: Carey, Lea and Blanchard, 1836).

38. *Living,* op. cit. n. 36, p. 11.

39. Ibid., p. 23. He was aware by the time of this commencement sermon, 1878, that the distinctive stress of the Universalists had pretty much come to prevail in other denominations. Hence, said he, "we may be in danger of being too popular," ibid., p. 24. He therefore raised the question before the graduating seminarians of the distinctive mission of Universalist ministers, given the general diffusion of their chief doctrine, and fell back upon the Whitsuntide theme of the diversity of gifts of the Holy Spirit and called upon the graduates to magnify their future office as ambassadors of the Living God—in a concluding reference to his text from I Timothy 3:15.

40. *Proceedings,* op. cit. n. 13, p. 91A.

41. Ibid., p. 91A.

42. Ibid., p. 89A.

43. Ibid., p. 92B.

44. Ibid., p. 92A. The reference to Christ's death for the churchless and the skeptics again picks up in muted form Murray's conception of Christ's universally atoning death. See above at n. 13 and n. 19 in the Introduction.

45. Ibid., p. 92AB.

46. His life was placed in a romantically heroic setting (with disproportionate allusions to great figures and episodes in classical, scriptural, and Christian history somewhat like Cotton Mather in his grandiloquent *Magnalia Christi Americana*) by his son, Elbridge Streeter Brooks, *The Life-Work of Elbridge Gerry Brooks* (Boston: Universalist Publishing House, 1881). The son was a well-known novelist for juveniles. Dr. Brooks was roughly the counterpart in Universalism of Henry Whitney Bellows in Unitarianism.

47. Ibid., pp. 160–171.

48. *G. C. Minutes 1870,* op. cit. n. 1, p. 6.

49. Ibid., pp. 53–95.

50. Completed for the denominational press in Boston belatedly (partly because of growing blindness) for publication in 1874, though conceived in 1871. The volume aroused a storm of acrimonious protest within the denomination, *Life-Work,* op. cit. n. 46, pp. 184f.

51. Members of both local entities were expected to give "expressed assent" to the Winchester Confession of Faith. The constitution for the parish is to be found in *G. C. Minutes 1870,* op. cit. n. 1, pp. 81–84; that of the church, pp. 84–88.

52. Above at n.18 in the Introduction and n. 34, ch. 1.

53. *Our New Departure: or, the Methods and Work of the Universalist Church of America, as It Enters on Its Second Century* (Boston: Universalist Publishing House, 1874), pp. 250f.

54. Ibid., p. 234.

55. Ibid., p. 244, repeated by E. S. Brooks in *Life-Work,* op. cit. n. 46, p. 183.

56. Ibid., p. 238. Brooks was here thinking primarily of the kind of evangelical Protestantism from which he himself had come, Baptists and revivalistic sectarian congregationalists of various kinds rather than of Episcopalians, Methodists, Presbyterians, et al.

57. Ibid., p. 238.

58. Ibid., p. 235.

59. Ibid., p. 232.

60. Ibid., p. 244: "[W]e might with great profit relieve the barrenness of our

Protestant church edifices by the introduction of appropriate pictures and statuary."

61. Ibid., p. 244.
62. Ibid., p. 237: "Some of the sweetest and saintliest lives that have ever blossomed amidst the selfishness . . . of the world."
63. Ibid., p. 245.
64. Ibid., p. 237.
65. Ibid., p. 237.
66. Ibid., p. 237. He goes on: "to say nothing of the lawlessness and barbarism of large numbers whom it forces to hold, or of the pauperism and crime with which it is so shockingly flooding our American society."
67. Ibid., pp. 244f.
68. Ibid., p. 239, italics mine.
69. Ibid., p. 239.
70. Ibid., p. 246.
71. Ibid., pp. 248f. Mention may be made here of the denominational manual *The Church* (Boston: Universalist Publishing House, 1891) written in the spirit of Brooks by Henry Warren Rugg.
72. Ibid., p. 248. "Mutual watchfulness" is a gentle term for the work of the committee on discipline in the denomination from the association level up to that of the General Convention. We will note its operation on that level in 1872 in the disfellowshipping of Herman Bisbee, below at n. 94 in this chapter. In the earlier period one can see the importance of the committee on discipline in the discountenancing or disfellowshipping of itinerant ministers and others on the association level in the no doubt representative minutes of the Western Reserve Association, Ohio, 1832–1853, Universalist Historical Library (UHL), Ohio No. 19, pp. 33, 36, 49.
73. Cf. as late as 1828 in Boston, *The Right of Universalists to Testify in a Court of Justice Vindicated.* The animated participation of Universalists, clerical and lay, in political life must be further attended to. A large thrust in nationalist Universalism can be made to fit into the larger picture of the Messianic Nation. It is to be regretted that the denomination is never dealt with, sometimes never even mentioned in such comprehensive topical works as Ernest Lee Tuveson, *Redeemer Nation: The Idea of the American Millennial Role* (Chicago: University of Chicago Press, 1968), Martin Marty, *The Righteous Empire* (New York: Dial Press, 1970), and Ernest Sandeen, *The Roots of Fundamentalism: British and American Millenarianism, 1800–1930* (Chicago: University of Chicago Press, 1970). The close association of Universalists with the International Order of Odd Fellows, from 1819 on, over against the Masonic Order, also needs inves-

tigation. Both had British antecedents. Both had political as well as fraternal significance.

74. *Proceedings,* op. cit. n. 13, pp. 59–61, esp. p. 59A. For his wartime mood, see his "The Logic and the End of the Rebellion," *The Universalist Quarterly and General Review, I* (1844), pp. 1–15. For his life, see *In Memoriam Israel Washburn, Jr.* (privately printed, 1884).

75. This distinction and terminology go back to a book embodying the lectures of Woodbury M. Fernald at Newburyport, MA, *Universalism Against Partialism* (Boston: Mussey, 1840), esp. p. iv. The "evangelists" E. E. Guild and L. H. Hyatt in *The Universalist's Book of Reference* (Boston: Universalist Publishing House, 1853) refer to Partialists in the body of their work, p. 409, but have another designation in their subtitle: "Limitarians and Universalists." John Murray, of course, spoke of the "partial Saviour" and the "partial gospel" in his *Life of Rev. John Murray,* op. cit. n. 34, p. 263. It is not certain who first exploited for Universalist–Partialist terminology the account in Acts 10:34f of the faith of the Roman centurion and God's expressly showing "no partiality" and therefore disapproving Partialism.

76. *Proceedings,* op. cit. n. 13, p. 60.

77. Ibid., p. 60A.

78. Ibid., p. 60.

79. Ibid., p. 61A.

80. Italics mine; *G. C. Minutes 1889,* op. cit. n. 1, quoted in full in *Universalism in America,* op. cit. n. 8, vol. 2, p. 359.

81. Murray was named chaplain by the commanding officer of the Rhode Island Brigade stationed at the time in Cambridge and confirmed in the appointment by Washington. Roy J. Honeywell, *Chaplains of the United States Army* (Washington, DC: Office of the Chief of Chaplains, Department of the Army, 1958), p. 43.

82. By the Reverend A. J. Patterson in a centenary celebration in Portsmouth, New Hampshire, *Centennial Anniversary of the Planting of Universalism in Portsmouth, N.H., November 16 & 17, 1873* (Portsmouth, NH: William A. Plaisted, 1873), p. 70, and *Universalist Quarterly, XI.* Patterson, at the time of the Gloucester Centennial, was a ministerial delegate from Boston Highlands, Massachusetts.

83. Italics mine, ibid., pp. 63, 60. The last phrase echoes Canticles 6:4, 10 and also John Bunyan's use thereof and resonates with eschatological overtones. The strong word *cripple* gives as good occasion as any to remark that a much needed study is that of the extensive polemical literature that grew up between Universalists and a range of Protestant groups from Millerites to United Brethren. Such a study with all the numerous local

and regional debates calendared and analyzed would be an important index to Universalist impact and an immensely interesting account, which has been virtually overlooked by both Universalists and others despite the rows of faded volumes of animated debate.

84. Mary A. Livermore has left an immense, profusely illustrated autobiography, *The Story of My Life or the Sunshine and Shadows of Seventy Years* (A. D. Worthington, 1898). Chapters viii–xxi recount her experiences among Virginia slaveholders and could be reprinted in the interest of black studies. She is sketched by Eliza Rice Hanson, *Our Woman Workers: Biographical Sketches of Women Eminent in the Universalist Church for Literary, Philanthropic, and Christian Work* (Chicago: The Star and Covenant Office, 1882), pp. 120–124.

85. Her Thursday morning speech is printed in *Centennial,* op. cit. n. 82, pp. 61–64, this passage p. 62A.

86. Before the Women's Centenary Aid Association, ibid., pp. 53–58.

87. Ibid., p. 54B.

88. Ibid., p. 56A.

89. Quotations seriatim from the Wednesday speech, ibid., pp. 56A–57B. The Reverend Thomas Abbott had once edited a monthly out of Indianapolis and St. Louis, entitled *The Golden Age.*

90. *Centennial,* op. cit. n. 82, p. 62B.

91. Ibid., p. 63A.

92. Ibid., p. 63B.

93. That those who have been styled exponents of Christian Universalism shared also in the nationalist ideal is evidenced, for example, by E. H. Chapin's *True Patriotism* (Boston: Abel Tompkins, 1847) and *The American Idea and What Grows Out of It* (Boston: Abel Tompkins, 1854).

94. See Marty F. Bogue, a descendant, "The Minneapolis Radical Lectures and the Excommunication of the Reverend Herman Bisbee," *JUHS, VII* (1967–68), pp. 3–69. Bisbee himself wrote the biography of his predecessor at St. Anthony, *Memoir of Rev. Seth Barnes* (Cincinnati: Williamson and Cantwell, 1868), dedicated "to the Universalists of the West."

95. A composite of three paragraphs taken from an already contracted version of the sermon printed by Bogue, "Minneapolis," ibid., pp. 12f.

96. Eddy gives a detailed account, "The Restorationist Controversy, 1817–1841," in *Universalism in America,* op. cit. n. 8, vol. 2, pp. 260–342. Frederic Perkins supplies a compact summary, *Beliefs Commonly Held Among Us* (Boston: Universalist Church of America, 1945).

97. Adin Ballou, "Restorationist Association," *The Universalist* (25 February 1871); quoted by Eddy in *Universalism in America,* ibid., see especially

pp. 336, 338. Cf. the Probationary controversy among the Congregationalists. It should be noted that Adin had been drawn to Universalism from
the Christian Connexion, which had promoted as scriptural the view that
at death unrepentant souls are annihilated.

98. Adin Ballou's *History of Hopedale* (Lowell, MA: Thompson and Hill, 1897)
and his *Autobiography of Adin Ballou, 1803–1890 with Appendixes* (Lowell,
MA: Thompson and Hill, 1896) were completed and edited by his son-
in-law, William S. Heywood.

See further Barbara L. Faulkner, "Adin Ballou and the Hopedale Com-
munity," Ph.D. dissertation, Boston University, Boston, 1985; William O.
Reichert, "The Philosophical Anarchism of Adin Ballou," *Huntington Li-
brary Quarterly, XXVII* (1964), pp. 357–374; and Lewis Perry, "Adin
Ballou's Hopedale Community and the Theology of Antislavery," *Church
History, XXXIX* (1970), pp. 372–389.

99. The second and third volumes of Ballou's lectures were edited posthumously by William S. Heywood in "Christian Sociology," *Primitive Christianity and Its Corruptions* (Lowell, MA: Thompson and Hill, 1900). The
lectures constituting the third volume were delivered in Hopedale, 1871–
1872.

100. Vol. 3, p. 466.

101. Ibid., p. 463.

102. Ibid., p. 459 for the statement of the doctrine and p. 460 for the idea of its
universal Permeation.

103. Italics his, ibid., p. 468.

104. Ibid., p. 110, item 3.

105. Ibid., p. 115, items 8 and 6.

106. Ibid., p. 478.

107. Ibid., p. 118.

108. Ibid., p. 480.

Selected Aspects of American Universalism in Bicentennial Perspective

1. The accent in this section and the one to follow is on the period after
1870, but earlier concerns for reform will be amply alluded to.

2. *Proceedings at the Universalist Centennial Held in Gloucester, Massachusetts, September 20th, 21st, and 22nd, 1870* (Boston: Universalist Publishing House, 1870), pp. 102–104. Here is the place to remark that much
research needs to be done on the history of the Murray Press, on the hym-
nals and books on and for religious education, and especially on the wide
range of periodicals. The large list of periodicals in Richard Eddy, *Univer-*

salism in America, vol. 2 (Boston: Universalist Publishing House, 1886), pp. 589–99, indicates that there were 181 started between 1793 and 1888. This list should be completed to 1961 with addenda and annotations. Universalists were enormously interested in getting things published, from sermons to autobiographies.

3. Horace Greeley, *Recollections of a Busy Life* (New York: J. B. Ford, 1869).

4. Ibid., *p. 70.*

5. "Letter from Hon. Horace Greeley," New York, February 10, 1855, to *The Christian Ambassador, V* February 17, 1855); reprinted by James Parton, *The Life of Horace Greeley* (Boston: J. R. Osgood and Co., 1872), pp. 523f.; see also Don C. Seitz, *Horace Greeley: Founder of the New York Tribune* (Indianapolis: Bobbs-Merrill, 1926), pp. 23–27. See also Richard Eddy, *The Life of Thomas J. Sawyer, S.T.D., LL.D. and of Caroline M. Sawyer* (Boston: Universalist Publishing House, 1900).

6. From an unidentified letter to a correspondent as cited by Seitz in *Horace Greeley*, ibid., p. 320.

7. Letter of 1855, cf. *Horace Greeley*, ibid., ch. 6.

8. *Faith with Power: A Life Story of Quillen Hamilton Shinn, D.D.* by William H. McGlauflin, general superintendent (1907–1917) (Boston: Universalist Publishing House, 1912) does not give an integrated account, although it contains many interesting letters. Emerson Hugh Lalone (d. 1960), *And Thy Neighbor as Thyself: A Story of Universalist Social Action* (Boston: Universalist Publishing House 1939), ch. 7, places him in the context of Universalist social action.

9. The antecedent expression of denominational social reform had been the Universalist Reform Association of Massachusetts from 1846 to 1883, *And Thy Neighbor*, ibid., ch. 5, esp. pp. 39f.

10. Letter from Beverly, West Virginia, September 23, 1861, in *Faith*, op. cit. n. 8, p. 18. Shinn greatly exaggerated losses on both sides.

11. Dr. Vincent E. Tomlinson, "The Missionary Movement of the Last Fifty Years," *One Hundred and Fiftieth Anniversary of the Founding of Universalism in America, Stenographic Record* (1920), p. 25. This typescript lacks the major speeches, which appear with editorial matter in Dr. Fredrick A. Bisbee, ed., *1770–1920: From Good Luck to Gloucester: The Book of Pilgrimage* (Boston: Murray Press, 1920). The stenographic account on p. 26 supplies a statement from the floor as to Shinn's presence at Gloucester.

12. The Quillen Shinn Memorial Church in Chattanooga commemorated one of his most successful foundations in the South. Recent titles on Universalism in the South are John E. Williams, *A History of Universalism in North Carolina* (Rose Hill, NC: Universalist Convention of North Caro-

lina, 1968); G. Wayman McCarty, "A History of the Universalist Church in the Mid-South," M.A. thesis, Mississippi State University (Oxford, MS 1904); and David A. Johnson, "Beginnings of Universalism in Louisville," *The Filson Club History Quarterly, XLIII* (1969), pp. 173–83.

13. In the year of the publication the First Chapel of the Pines was set up at Ferry Beach (not far from the main Ferry Park House called "The Quillen") with these words: "I am the bearer of good tidings—We believe in the Universal Fatherhood of God, We believe in the Spiritual Leadership of Jesus, We believe in the doctrine of Brotherly Love and the Abundant Life, We believe in the Final Harmony of All Souls with God." A picture of the chapel and the missioner are to be found in Harold C. Perham, *The Maine Book of Universalism* (Norway, ME: The Advertiser Democrat, 1953), pp. 2, 162, 164; see also Robert Francis Needham and Katherine A. Sutton, eds., *The Universalists at Ferry Beach* (Boston: Universalist Publishing House, 1948).

14. Quillen H. Shinn, "Affirmation of Universalism," in *Good Tidings* (Boston: Universalist Publishing House, 1900), p. 78.

15. Ibid., p. 73.

16. Ibid., p. 74.

17. Ibid., p. 82.

18. Italics his, ibid., p. 84.

19. Ibid., p. 81.

20. Ibid., p. 69.

21. Ibid., pp. 71–73.

22. Ibid., pp. 87f. His images drawn from nature are particularly beautiful and in line with a clear impulse from Romantic John Murray himself.

23. Besides the Gloucester Centennial of 1870, there were other Universalist centennial publications about this time from which we may gain a solid sense of what the whole denomination was like just one hundred years ago. Such a collective work is Abel C. Thomas, ed., *A Century of Universalism in Philadelphia and New York* (Philadelphia: Collins, 1872).

24. The basic fact here, of course, is that John Murray both loved and hated his very pious and stern Methodist father, whose place he eventually took in the still-young family, governing in a sense even his widowed mother and assuming his father's place in family prayer from the deathbed transfer of authority on. But then there was also the rather extraordinary experience of young Murray's having been adopted into the family of a well-to-do neighboring family as an express replacement of their son, John's very close friend, who had died of brain fever. John Murray's frequent reference to the "God of my father," his feeling of his earthly father's

having been replaced by the heavenly Father, his prayerful address to England after returning to it from Ireland as "parent earth," his likening himself to "the universal parent," Adam, are but some of the rather unusual clustering of filial-paternal emotions to be found in his writings. John Murray, *The Life of Rev. John Murray*, centennial ed. (Boston: Munroe and Francis, 1870), pp. 89, 93, 103, 190, 194.

25. "A Hundred Years," *The Christian Register*, XLIX (September 1870), reprinted in *Proceedings*, op. cit. n. 2, p. 109B.

26. *Proceedings*, op. cit. n. 2, pp. 52f. See most recently Catherine F. Hitchings, *Universalist and Unitarian Women Ministers* (Boston: Universalist Historical Society, 1975), p. 53.

27. Obituary, *The Universalist Leader*, VIII (1905), p. 884.

28. Eliza Rice Hanson, *Our Woman Workers: Biographical Sketches of Women Eminent in the Universalist Church for Literary, Philanthropic, and Christian Work* (Chicago: The Star and Covenant Office, 1882).

29. Ibid., p. v.

30. Ibid., p. vi.

31. Ibid., p. vii.

32. *Proceedings*, op. cit. n. 2, p. 57B.

33. Ibid., p. 57A. The preceding paraphrases the thrust of her implied comparison between a mother's love for her child at every stage even unto untimely death and God's unswervable purpose to seek the lost sheep until he finds it. Cf. p. 56B.

34. The reference here is to the second Mrs. Murray, the widow Judith Sargent Stevens of Gloucester whom he married in 1788, and who later edited his autobiography in 1816 and died in 1820. The first Mrs. Murray, Eliza Neale of London, died in 1768. It was in her uncle's home that John Murray picked up a copy of James Relly's *Union* or *A Treatise of the Consanguinity between Christ and His Church* (Boston: White and Adams, 1779). He had already been exposed to it negatively. It was Eliza Neale who more perceptively, swiftly, and courageously accepted Relly's universalism and encouraged her husband therein. *The Life of Rev. John Murray*, op. cit. n. 24, p. 145.

35. Antoinette L. Brown was congregationally (and ecumenically) ordained in 1853 in the Orthodox Congregational Church of South Butler, New York. She was once proposed with levity as a compromise candidate for Congress chaplain.

36. Our principal source is "An Autobiography," edited and completed by her daughter, Gwendolen B. Willis, *Journal of the Universalist Historical Society*, IV, (1963), pp. 1–76, with a reprint of two chapters from Olympia

Brown, *Acquaintances, Old and New, Among Reformers* (privately printed 1911) and two reconstructed sermons. There is further bibliographical reference in *Journal of the Universalist Historical Society, V* (1964–65), p. 123.

37. "Autobiography," ibid., p. 24.

38. The Racine *Sunday Bulletin* (April 8, 1962), p. 6A, noted in the "Autobiography," ibid., p. iii.

39. Phineas Taylor Barnum, who began his career as an abolitionist and ticket seller, was a good friend also of both Dr. Chapin and Horace Greeley, all three of whom were at the Centennial Convention. In 1871 he would inaugurate the "Greatest Show on Earth," his three-ring circus, and the humorously deceptive "This way to the Egress!" Barnum later gave a building to Tufts College bearing the inscription "Barnum Fecit." His oft-printed and ever updated autobiography and his popular Universalist tract, *Why I Am a Universalist,* gave among other things his interesting views about continuous effort and growth in the afterlife.

40. Her husband was John Henry Willis.

41. See Alan Seaburg, "Missionary to Scotland: Caroline Augusta Soule," *Transactions of the Unitarian Historical Society, XIV*, No. 1 (1967), pp. 28–41.

42. They would be the first denominations to go on record, in 1929, in favor of contraception and the abolition of laws interfering with its public and private implementation. *And Thy Neighbor,* op cit. n. 8, p. 89.

43. Besides the extensive bibliography, see also the brief vivid account of Robert S. Wolley, "Clara Barton, A Biographical Sketch of Compulsion," *Journal of the Universalist Historical Society, I* (1959), pp. 11–31, wherein it is recognized: "Clara Barton is a mystery."

44. Letter to Mrs. Jennie Vinton of Oxford, on the occasion of the rededication of the church, October 1904—pamphlet, Universalist Historical Library. The Oxford church, built in 1793, vies with that of Gloucester (1780) for the honor of being the oldest of the denomination. Clara's father was fighting with "Mad Anthony" Wayne in the West, 1793–1796. Percy H. Epler, *The Life of Clara Barton* (New York: MacMillan, 1915), pp. 3–7. Conventions may have been held as early as 1785.

45. *[Early] Life,* Universalist Historical Library.

46. A phrenologist, consulted when she was fifteen, advised, "She will never assert herself for herself; she will suffer wrong first. But for others she will be perfectly fearless. Throw responsibility upon her, give her a school to teach!" *Life of Clara Barton,* op. cit. n. 44, p. 18.

47. Her single and assertive leadership, however, proved something of a hindrance to the organization, which grew most significantly only after her resignation in 1904.

48. Cf. resolution, *Minutes of the General Convention* (New York, 1874), p. 9.

49. "Autobiography," op. cit. n. 36, pp. 45–63, which simply recasts *Acquaintances*, pp. 75–79.

50. *Minutes of the General Convention* (Minneapolis, 1905), p. 108.

51. Cf. *Minutes of the General Convention* (Akron, OH, 1886), p. 8; *G. C. Minutes 1905*, ibid., pp. 108–09; *Minutes of the General Convention* (Philadelphia, 1907), p. 101.

52. *G. C. Minutes 1907*, ibid., p. 11.

53. *Minutes of the General Convention* (Detroit, 1909), p. 16.

54. *Minutes of the General Convention* (Springfield, MA, 1911), pp. 14f.

55. *Minutes of the General Convention* (Philadelphia, 1882), p. 4.

56. *Minutes of the General Convention* (Providence, RI, 1878), p. 9, justified the restriction on the ground "that the use of fermented wine at the Communion has the effect of keeping from the table of the Lord (either from conscientious scruples or from the fear of the results of a single taste of the fermented wine upon an appetite which needs but a spark to place it beyond control) many who would be glad to strengthen their religious convictions by this service."

57. *G. C. Minutes 1878*, ibid., p. 9.

58. Now conjectured to be 1784 by L. H. Butterfield, editor of the Rush letters. There was an exposition by Hosea Starr Ballou of the religion of Dr. Rush, "Ideal Universalist Layman," *G. C. Minutes 1907*, op. cit. n. 51, pp. 105–115.

59. *Minutes of the General Convention*, (New York, 1885), p. 7.

60. The 1923 resolution on law enforcement specifically refers to the Prohibition Amendment, *Minutes of the General Convention* (1923), p. 37. While *Minutes of the General Convention* (1929), pp. 22–23, and *Minutes of the General Convention 1931*, *Yearbook* (Boston: Universalist General Convention, 1932), p. 19, are more general calls for obedience to the law.

61. L. H. Butterfield, ed., *Letters of Benjamin Rush*, vol. 1 (Princeton, NJ: Princeton University Press, 1951), p. 272, n. 3.

62. *Letters of Benjamin Rush*, ibid., vol. 2, pp. 976–79, September 10, 1808.

63. *Minutes of the General Convention* (1790) in Universalist Historical Library.

64. *Letters of Benjamin Rush*, op. cit. n. 61, vol. 2, pp. 754–758; E. M. Stone, *Biography of Elhanan Winchester* (Boston: H. B. Brewster, 1836).

65. *Biography of Elhanan Winchester*, ibid., was reprinted as *Reverend Elhanan Winchester: Biography and Letters* (New York: Arno Press, 1972).

66. Adin Ballou, *Autobiography of Adin Ballou, 1803–1890 with Appendixes*, ed. by William S. Heywood (Lowell, MA: Thompson and Hill, 1896), pp. 277–287; Lewis Perry, "Adin Ballou's Hopedale Community and the

Theology of Antislavery." *Church History, XXXIX* (1970), pp. 375, 387, 389.

67. Elmo Robinson, *The Universalist Church in Ohio* (privately printed, 1923), pp. 123f.

68. John G. Adams, *Fifty Notable Years* (Boston: Universalist Publishing House, 1883), p. 65.

69. Cf. *Minutes of the General Convention* (Lynn, MA, 1889), p. 8.

70. *Theology of Universalism* (Boston: Universalist Publishing House, 1862).

71. Abel C. Thomas, *Autobiography* (Boston: J. M. Usher, 1852), p. 217.

72. *And Thy Neighbor*, op. cit. n. 8, p. 89.

73. The Universalist minister, Charles N. Leonard, then of Chelsea, Massachusetts (later theological dean at Tufts), founded Children's Day. But child labor was first condemned by the General Convention as a whole in a resolution of 1907, *G. C. Minutes 1907*, op. cit. n. 51, p. 101, nearly thirty years after Massachusetts had passed the first child labor legislation in 1879.

74. *Minutes of the General Convention* (Peoria, IL, 1884), p. 7.

75. *The Christian Leader, LXIV*, No. 19 (May 1894), p. 2.

76. Cf. *Minutes of the General Convention* (Worcester, MA, 1891), p. 9.

77. *Universalist Leader, III* (September 12, 1900), p. 1196.

78. Tributes with a picture are gathered up in *Memory Book: Rev. James Minton Pullman, D.D.* (privately published, 1904).

79. Stanley Buder, *Pullman: An Experiment in Industrial Order and Community Planning, 1880–1930* (New York: Oxford University Press, 1967).

80. See Colston E. Warne, ed., *The Pullman Boycott of 1894* (Boston: Heath, 1955).

81. For example, Joseph Pulitzer's *New York World* was condemned as religiously "worldly" over against the high paternalistic vision of the Pullmans.

82. *Christian Leader, LXIV*, no. 21 (May 24, 1894), p. 4. The ceremony was attended not only by the three Pullmans mentioned and their immediate families, but also by their sisters, Mrs. George West and Mrs. W. F. Fluhrer. The latter was evidently related in some way to the first pastor of the church, the Reverend Charles Fluhrer. See *Universalist Leader, V*, no. 46 (January 11, 1902).

83. He had married a niece of George M. Pullman. See obituary, *Universalist Leader, V*, no. 657 (May 24, 1902).

84. *Christian Leader, LXIV*, no. 29 (July 19, 1894), pp. 1, 4.

85. "The Pullman Strike," *Christian Leader, LXIV*, no. 30 (July 26, 1894), p. 1.

86. Cf. his sermon, *The Moral Aspects of the Present Campaign* (October 4, 1896) in Universalist Historical Library.

87. *Universalist Leader, VI*, no. 657 (May 24, 1902). It was Ballou's contention that the Drapers took over a going concern, which they then proceeded to exploit.

88. *Christian Leader, LXVII*, no. 43 (October 28, 1897), p. 12.

89. James M. Pullman, *Universalism and the New World-Problems* (Address to the General Assembly, 1901), pamphlet in the Universalist Historical Library, pp. 2–3. 90. "The Spiritual Needs of the Universalist Church," *The Universalist Leader, III* (1900), pp. 1581–1582. Much later in his life at a political event, Powers offered a most forthright and humorous prayer, widely reprinted, last of all in *Reader's Digest*.

91. See the commission's first reports, *G. C. Minutes 1911*, op. cit. n. 54, pp. 96–101, and *Minutes of the General Convention* (Chicago 1913), pp. 80–92.

92. Reprinted with an interpretive introduction by James D. Hunt, *Journal of the Universalist Historical Society, V* (1964–65), pp. 79–122, and again as Beacon Reference Series No. 4 (Boston: Beacon Press, 1966).

93. *And Thy Neighbor*, op. cit. n. 8, pp. 109–112.

94. Ibid., p. 112. Only in 1937, however, did the General Convention finally endorse the principle of collective bargaining, *Minutes of the General Convention* (Chicago, 1937), p. 21. See further the updated "Affirmation of Social Principles" adopted in *Minutes of the General Convention* (New York, 1943), pp. 30–32.

95. Ida M. Tarbell, *Owen Young* (New York: MacMillan, 1932), pp. 125–28; 294.

96. Quoted by James D. Hunt in his vivid "The Social Gospel as a Way of Life: A Biography of H. C. Ledyard, Universalist Minister and Labor leader, 1880–1950," *Journal of the Universalist Historical Society, V* (1964–65), pp. 31–63, passage p. 32.

97. *The Life of Rev. John Murray*, op. cit. n. 24, pp. 272, 294, 373.

98. The interest in gardens, flowers, birds, forests, and scenery is evident in his autobiography, ibid., pp. 89, 92, 104f., 109, 194, 346. His belief in the restitution of all things to final harmony must have been the basis for the report "that he believed that his little canine companion would one day wag his tail in glory" (Daniel Bragg Clayton, *Forty-Seven Years in the Universalist Ministry*, 1889, p. 89. The reference cannot be to the autobiography. It may be in Murray's three volumes of sketches and correspondence. More likely it was simply a general account. Joseph Priestley also believed in a future restitution for animals. The feeling for nature among Universalists and their concern to minimize cruelty to animals, as evidenced in articles, newspaper columns, and curricula, are so prominent in the sources that further study here could be instructive. Surely the restitution of all

(Acts 3:21) and the Gospel to all Creatures (Mark 16:15) must have played a role more pronounced in Universalism than in other denominations.

99. *Fifty,* op. cit. n. 68, p. 75.

100. Preface, *Good Tidings,* op. cit. n. 14, pp. 5f. The essay introduced by Shinn was that of the Reverend Charles H. Puffer, "Capital Punishment," ibid., pp. 104–134. Puffer dealt first carefully and critically with the biblical texts and concluded "that the Bible does not command that magistrates of to-day exact life for life" and then went on to sociological, psychological, and humane anthropological arguments.

101. *One Hundred and Fifty Years of Universalism,* pamphlet (Boston, c. 1920), p. 6.

102. *Minutes of the General Convention 1882,* op. cit. n. 55, p. 5. Quinby also wrote *Heaven Our Home: The Christian Doctrine of the Resurrection, Showing Man the Victor over Death and Sin* (Augusta, ME: Gospel Banner Office, 1876).

103. Letter to Jeremy Belknap, *Letters of Benjamin Rush,* op. cit. n. 61, vol. 1, pp. 583–584. Rush's tract on the subject of capital punishments was first published in the *American Museum, IV* (July 1783) pp. 78–82 and later expanded as *Considerations on the Injustice and Impolicy of Punishing Murder by Death,* (Philadelphia: Matthew Carey, 1792).

104. In his weekly, which Whittemore edited in Boston, *Trumpet and Universalist Magazine.*

105. John Murray Spear, *Labors for the Prisoners* (Boston, 1849). He and his brother edited *Voices from Prison: Being a Selection of Poetry from Various Prisoners, Written within the Cell* (Boston: C. and J. M. Spear, 1847).

106. Universalist experience of and interest in spiritualism and related matters is sufficiently prominent in the sources to deserve attention in a section of its own rather than *en passant* in connection with penology! Mention should be made of the instances of telepathy, clairvoyance, visions, spiritual presences, etc. in *Life of Rev. John Murray,* op. cit. n. 24, pp. 87, 180, 191, 200, 205, 251. And Elhanan Winchester provided a recommendatory preface to Dr. George de Benneville's *A True and Remarkable Account of the Life and Trance of George de Benneville* (Norristown, PA: David Sower, 1800), reprinted in full by Ernest Cassara, *Journal of the Universalist Historical Society,* vol. 2 (1960–61), pp. 71–87.

107. "Crime, Capital Punishment, Intemperance," *Columbian Universalist Congress* (1893), ch. 23.

108. *Life of Rev. John Murray,* op. cit. n. 24, pp. 35–37.

109. These were edited by S. C. Hewitt, Boston, 1853.

110. Orestes Brownson, *The Spirit-Rapper: An Autobiography* (Boston: Little,

Brown, 1854).

111. Frank Podmore, *Modern Spiritualism*, 2 vols. (London: Methuen, 1902), republished with a new introduction as *Mediums of the 19th Century* (New Hyde Park, NY: University Books, 1963), with reference to J. M. Spear and other Universalists, vol. 1, pp. 217, 219ff.; vol. 2, p. 351. See also John M. Spear, *The Educator: Being Suggestions . . . Designed to Promote Man-culture and Integral Reforms, with a View to the Ultimate Establishment of a Divine Social State on Earth: Comprised in a Series of Revealments from Organised Associations in the Spirit-life* (Boston: Office of Practical Spiritualists, 1857).

112. In view of the interest in Spiritualism on the part of a number of Universalists, 1844–1907, it is not surprising to find a greeting to the General Convention of 1903 from the National Spiritualist Association. Percy H. Epler, *Life of Clara Barton*, op. cit. n. 44 (New York: MacMillan, 1915), pp. 470f; *Minutes of the General Convention* (Washington, DC 1903), p. 112.

113. Clinton Lee Scott, *The Universalist Church of America* (Boston: Universalist Historical Society, 1957), p. 89.

114. *G. C. Minutes 1899*, op. cit. n. 69, pp. 16–17; *Minutes of the General Convention* (Chicago, 1897), pp. 16f.

115. *Letters* (1895–1905), p. 108, in the Universalist Historical Library.

116. Charles Dudley Warner.

117. *Minutes of the General Convention, 1870* (New York: J. Sutton and Co., 1871), p. 15.

118. *Minutes of the General Convention* (1875), p. 10. The relationship between L. J. Fletcher and Austin Barclay Fletcher (d. 1923), benefactor of the Fletcher School of Law and Diplomacy of Tufts University, if any, has not been determined.

119. *G. C. Minutes 1885*, op. cit. n. 59, p. 6.

120. *G. C. Minutes 1889*, op. cit. n. 69, p. 8; *G. C. Minutes 1891*, op. cit. n. 76, p. 74.

121. *Minutes of the General Convention* (Washington, DC, 1893), pp. 12, 54.

122. *G. C. Minutes 1905*, op. cit. n. 50, p. 108. Cf. also *G. C. Minutes 1907*, op. cit. n. 51, pp. 100–101; *G. C. Minutes 1909*, op. cit. n. 53, p. 98; *G. C. Minutes 1911*, op. cit. n. 54, p. 14.

123. *Minutes of the General Convention* (Philadelphia, 1790), Universalist Historical Library, reprinted in *And Thy Neighbor*, op. cit. n. 8.

124. Peter Brock, *Pacifism in the United States* (Princeton: Princeton University Press, 1958), p. 712.

125. Adin Ballou, *Autobiography* (Lowell, MA: Thompson and Hill, 1896), pp. 108f., 126f.

126. Ibid., p. 187.

127. Ibid., pp. 277–278. Cf. the account of his address on "the great system of American oppression," p. 283, July 4, 1837.

128. Ibid., p. 306.

129. James D. Hunt has shown not only the mutual influence of Ballou and Tolstoy but also the great admiration of Tolstoy for Ballou as a predecessor, hailing the American pacifist, despite certain qualifications, as "one of the first true apostles of the 'New Time.'" Hunt shows further that, by way of Tolstoy, Ballou's influence was also felt by Mahatma Gandhi in "Gandhi, Thoreau, and Adin Ballou," *Journal of the Liberal Ministry,* IX, No. 3 (1969), esp. pp. 11–51.

130. Peter Brock, *Christian Non-Resistance* (Philadelphia: J. Miller M'Kim, 1846), p. 21.

131. *Autobiography,* op. cit. n. 125, pp. 88–96.

132. *Christian Non-Resistance,* op. cit. n. 130, p. 181, where he quotes at length from the *Manual of Peace* (New York: Leavitt, Lord, 1836) by Gilmanton, New Hampshire–born Bowdoin professor Thomas Cogswell Upham, Congregationalist ethicist to whom Charles Spear also dedicated his book.

133. *Christian Non-Resistance,* ibid., pp. 61–63 et passim. In contrast, most of his Christian opponents allegedly insisted on distinguishing the ethical demands of the New Testament from the still more exacting demands of the millennium.

134. John Gregory, *Two Anti-War Discourses* (Boston: C. C. Briggs, 1847), pp. 97–98. For consciousness of being primitive Christians in another geographical sector of the denomination, note the Michigan Universalist publication, *Expounder of Primitive Christianity,* 1843–1848.

135. In Massachusetts, in 1846, at the insistence of the Reverend C. H. Fay of Roxbury. It survived until 1863. Cf. *And Thy Neighbor,* op. cit. n. 8, pp. 39f.

136. *Anti-War,* op. cit. n. 134, pp. 8, 69, 94–96, 98, quoted by Brock in *Christian Non-Resistance,* op. cit. n. 130, p. 568; cf. an anonymous correspondent [Gregory?] to the *New York Christian Messenger* (June 6, 1846), quoted by Lalone in *And Thy Neighbor,* ibid., p. 38.

137. Brock, ibid., p. 568; cf. the defection of Garrison and others from the cause of nonresistance.

138. Cf. the action of Clara Barton and the American Red Cross in Cuba, *Life of Clara Barton,* op. cit. n. 44, ch. 33. Her description of the blowing up of the *Maine* glamorized Cuba for Universalists among others. Cf. articles by Superintendent I. M. Atwood in *The Universalist Leader,* II (1900), on Universalism in Cuba.

139. *Minutes of the General Convention* (Worcester, MA, 1917), p. 66.

140. Ibid., pp. 39–40.

141. Ibid., p. 49.

142. *And Thy Neighbor*, op. cit. n. 8, p. 89.

143. Ibid., p. 86.

144. *G. C. Minutes 1931*, op. cit. n. 60, p. 19.

145. *Minutes of the General Convention 1933, Yearbook* (Worcester, MA: Universalist General Convention, 1934), p. 13.

146. *And Thy Neighbor*, op. cit. n. 8, pp. 89–90 and appendix containing correspondence with the federal government, pp. 113–125.

147. The title of a symposium, edited by Dr. Henry W. Rugg of Providence, subtitled *A Series of Papers Treating of Principles and Ideas Relative to Christian Missions . . . with Special Reference to the Universalist Church* (Boston: Universalist Publishing House, 1894).

148. See Dr. G. L. Demerest, "The General Convention and Missions," *Word and Work*, vol. 5, esp. p. 100. It was before the Massachusetts Convention at the Weirs that a Japan mission was first bruited. Elmo Robinson, "The Universalist General Convention: From Nascence to Conjugation," *Journal of the Universalist Historical Society*, VIII (1969–70), p. 86.

149. *G. C. Minutes 1882*, op. cit. n. 55, p. 18, quoted by Demarest in *General Convention and Missions*, op. cit. n. 148, p. 99.

150. George Sumner Weaver, *James Henry Chapin: Sketches of His Life and Work* (New York: G. P. Putnam's Sons, 1894).

151. Lombard University gave him a kind of honorary Ph.D. in geology in June 1875 in recognition of his geographical and geological exploration and writing.

152. James Henry Chapin, *The Keys of the Kingdom of Heaven* (1875), p. 12.

153. Dr. Chapin's whole tour is described in *From Japan to Granada: Sketches of Observation and Inquiry in a Tour Round the World in 1887–1888* (New York: G. P. Putnam, 1889). On p. 51 he asks: "Is Christianity coming to fill the growing void . . . ?" and answers: "It is for the Christian churches of Europe and especially America to answer."

154. *G. C. Minutes 1886*, op. cit. n. 51, p. 9.

155. Ibid., p. 10. To be sure, the reference is expressly to infanticide, but Rexford must have had abortion in mind when speaking of a "vastly multiplied crime of *Christian* mothers." *The Universalist*, which would supply editorial commentary and clarification, for this year, is missing at the Universalist Historical Library. Individuals or churches in possession of venerable copies of this central repository of Universalist activity should notify the librarian for the sake of a general census and completion of the series at Tufts by xeroxing or gift depositions.

156. Editorial. "Concerning Our New Enterprise," *The Christian Leader*, January 16, 1890.

    For the peak in 1890, although Universalists at the time thought of theirs as the sixth largest denomination in the country, see Edwin Scott Gaustad, *Historical Atlas of Religion in America* (New York: Harper and Row, 1962), pp. 129–131. David Hicks MacPherson, on the basis of a close scrutiny of yearbooks from 1836 on, holds that the membership peaked in 1905, but that the peak in the number of societies reporting was in 1860 with 1,200. In 1870 it was down to 820. Correspondence with the author, August 30, 1971.

157. "Foreign Missionary Work: The Japanese Mission," in *Columbian Universalist Congress 1893* (1894), Paper XVIII, pp. 260–271, the quoted passage p. 268. Much the same article appears as "Our Mission in Japan," *Word and Work, VI*, with pictures.

158. Ibid., p. 264.

159. Ibid., p. 266.

160. Ibid., p. 261.

161. Ibid., p. 267.

162. "Our Mission," op. cit. n. 157, p. 109.

163. Italics mine, *Word and Work, II*, pp. 22–24.

164. Italics mine, "Christianity, a Universal Religion," *Word and Work, XI*, esp. pp. 187–190, passim.

165. Cf. the speech of Robert Cummins in 1943 quoted in *Excluded: The Story of the Council of Churches and the Universalists*, Beacon Reference Series, no. 3 (Boston: Beacon Press, 1964), p. i.

166. Already in 1894, the Reverend H. Hoskins, editor of the *Liberal Christian*, organ of the Japanese Universalists, had said much the same: "Many thoughtful men of our country are directly or indirectly in favor of Christianity, that is, in favor of its central ideas. But they do not like its complicated, ambiguous, and narrow doctrine. . . . Thoughtful men are hoping for and expecting under the Christian name a religion of power which shall satisfy the mind and heart, even as the Jewish people expected the coming of the Messiah. I believe the Universalist interpretation of Christianity—broad and reasonable as it is—will satisfy these waiting minds." "A Japanese View," *Word and Work, VII*, esp. pp. 130, 133.

167. The sense of decline is documented statistically and otherwise for two major state conventions: David H. MacPherson, "The Massachusetts Universalist Convention," *Journal of the Historical Universalist Society, VI* (1996), pp. 4–24; Richard M. Woodman, "The New York State Convention of Universalists," *Journal of the Historical Universalist Society, VI*, pp. 25–46.

168. Cf. Elmo Robinson, "Unrestricted Universalism," *Crozer Quarterly, XXIX* (1952), pp. 158–172.

169. Ibid., n. 10, Introduction.

170. *Christian Ambassador, X* (April 21, 1860); noted by Charles H. Vickery, "A Century of Rapprochement between the Universalist and Unitarian Churches," senior thesis, Tufts College School of Religion, Medford, MA, 1945, p. 17, Universalist Historical Library. I have not been able to consult a similar research paper by Peter Lee Scott, "A History of the Attempts of the Universalist and Unitarian Denominations to Unite," Theological School, St. Lawrence University, Canton, NY, 1957. For a similar bitter allusion circa 1861, see Erasmus Manford, quoted above in n. 11, Introduction.

171. "Universalists and Unitarians," *The Liberal Christian* (March 2, 1867), noted by Vickery in "Century," ibid., p. 18.

172. *Christian Register, LI*, no. 8 (February 10, 1872), p. 1, col. D, "Tribute to Universalism." The tribute seems to have been composed in connection with the Gloucester Centennial in 1870.

173. This was well before the Parliament, *Universalist Monthly,* November, 1891; "Century," op. cit. n. 170, p. 38.

174. *The New Unity, I* (June 21, 1894), p. 262; noted by Vickery in "Century," ibid., p. 33. The reference is to the three articles of the Winchester Profession of 1803.

175. *The New Unity, I*, 15 (June 12, 1895), p. 226; 16 (June 20, 1895). p. 241.

176. Pullman was quoting Pearl Andrews, *The New Unity, I*, no. 15 (June 12, 1895), p. 228; noted by Vickery in "Century," op. cit. n. 170, p. 31. One Universalist minister, A. N. Alcott of Elgin, Illinois, was disfellowshipped for working in the Congress mission. *Gospel Banner,* a periodical published in Augusta, ME, 1895.

177. E.g., in Dixon and in Chicago, Illinois. "Century," op. cit. n. 170, p. 34.

178. Quoted by Edwin C. Sweetser, "The Invitation of the American Unitarian Association," *The Universalist Leader, II*, no. 40 (Oct. 7, 1899), p. 8c (792). *The Non-Sectarian* published in St. Louis, 1891–1895.

179. *The Gospel Banner, LIX* (1893), quoted in "Century," op. cit. n. 170, p. 41.

180. *Minutes of the General Convention* (Meriden, CT, 1895), p. 69.

181. Ibid., p. 7.

182. Minutes of the Unitarian Association, 1899; *Christian Register, LXXVIII* (June 15, 1899), pp. 658f.

183. *Scrapbook*, Universalist Historical Library; quoted in "Century," op. cit. n. 170, p. 44.

184. For example, during the General Convention at Hudson, New York, he had sought unsuccessfully to substitute trinitarianizingly for article ii of

the Winchester Profession of Faith: "We believe that there is one *God*, whose nature is Love, revealed in one Lord *Jesus Christ*, by one *Holy Spirit* of Grace, who will finally save the whole family of mankind." *Minutes of the General Convention* (Hudson, NY, 1880), p. 9.

185. *The Universalist Leader, II*, No. 40 (Oct. 7, 1899), pp. 7e (791)–8c (792). He earlier wrote "Ought we to affiliate with the Unitarians?" *The Banner*, reprinted with approval and Southern applicability by *The Unitarian Herald* (Carson, GA), *XXX*, No. 10 (September 15, 1897); and by *The Christian Leader, LXVII*, No. 35 (September 2, 1897), p. 2.

186. Ibid., p. 7A (791A).

187. Ibid., p. 8C (792C).

188. *The Universalist Leader, III* (Sept. 1900); separately printed as a brochure, *Much Ado About Nothing*, iii.4.55 (Sept. 1901), and widely responded to.

189. *The Universalist Leader, II* (July 8, 1899), p. 7A-C (527 A-C).

190. But how different Perkins was from any contemporary Unitarian is evidenced in his article "Universalism, the Primitive Faith of the Early Christians," reprinted as late as 1953 in *Maine*, op. cit. n. 13, pp. 28–30.

191. *The Universalist Leader, II* (August 12, 1899), pp. 13A-14A (637A-638A).

192. Scott, *Short History*, p. 40. Elmo Robinson helpfully places the Boston Profession in the larger cycle, "Universalism, A Changing Faith," *Journal of the Universalist Historical Society, II* (1960–61), esp. pp. 13f.

193. This volume was a collection of essays that Cone in part translated himself from the German of Otto Pfleiderer. The doctrine of evolution was pretty widely accepted in the denomination by this time. See Cassara, "The Effect of Darwinism on Universalist Belief, *Journal of the Universalist Historical Society, I* (1959), pp. 32–42. Other works by Cone were *Gospel Criticism and Historical Christianity* (New York: G. P. Putnam,1891), followed by *The Gospel and its Earliest Interpretations* (New York: G. P. Putnam,1893) and *Paul* (New York: MacMillan,1898).

With his popular Minneapolis lectures Marion Shutter moved on to *Applied Evolution* (Boston, 1900).

194. In 1933 only one Universalist would sign the Humanist Manifesto (C. L. Scott). By 1935 the Universalist Church had become so much influenced by Darwinianism, biblical criticism, and the social gospel—directly and also indirectly through close association with the Unitarian denomination—that in the nonbinding *Great Avowal* or Bond of Fellowship and Statement of Faith in Washington the denomination would prove no longer to be Universalist in either the patristic-cosmological or the Calvinist-predestinarian sense. By then, "universalism" had undergone a third permutation, to be interpreted as universalized liberal Christianity

that understood itself as a one-world religion, prepared to seek common ground with other world religions. Scott, *Short History*, p. 40; "Changing Faith," op. cit. n. 192, pp. 14f. Charles Francis Potter, minister of a Humanist Society at the time, had been the Universalist minister of the Church of the Divine Paternity in New York until 1929 and was still in standing as a Universalist when he signed the Humanist Manifesto. *The Christian Leader*, XXXVI (1933), p. 661. He had written *Humanism: A New Religion* (New York: Simon and Schuster, 1930).

195. Tract No. 2, American Unitarian Association (circa 1901).
196. First serialized in *The Universalist Leader*, beginning April 10, 1901.
197. Joseph Henry Crooker, *The Church of Tomorrow* (Boston: Universalist Publishing House, 1911), pp. 8f.
198. *G. C. Minutes 1909*, op. cit. n. 53, p. 95.
199. Dr. Frederick A. Bisbee, ed., "Universalism and the Broad Church Movement in America," in *1770–1920: From Good Luck to Gloucester: The Book of Pilgrimage* (Boston: Murray Press, 1920), pp. 22–23.
200. J. G. Adams also wrote *The Christian Victor or, Mortality and Immortality Including Happy Death Scenes* (Boston: A. Tompkins, 1851).
201. See Roger F. Etz, "John Coleman Adams, Prophet of the Larger Faith," *The Christian Leader*, LII (December 1949), pp. 442–446. Adams expressed himself in *Universalism and the Universalist Church*, marking in 1922 the fiftieth anniversary (also the year of his death) of his ordination.
202. The motion for such a greeting came from Dr. Tomlinson. *G. C. Minutes 1913*, op. cit. n. 91, pp. 4f.
203. *Universalist Leader* (April 8, 1916), p. 9.
204. "A Message from the Congregational Church [sic]," *1770–1920*, op. cit. n. 199, pp. 338–347.
205. It is of passing interest that at their semi-centennial celebration in 1878 Maine Universalists were not then so open toward Congregationalists. When a resolution was offered expressing "sympathy and fellowship with the Congregational Conference" meeting concurrently in Auburn, some Universalist delegates retorted, "I don't want the Convention to appear as soliciting the graces of the Congregationlists"; "We lose our dignity"; "Let us plow our own furrow and leave results with Almighty God," quoted in "Against Universal Bigotry," *Maine*, op. cit. n. 13, pp. 108f.
206. *Minutes of the General Convention* (Syracuse, NY, 1925), p. 12.
207. *Minutes of the General Convention, 1927, Yearbook* (1928), p. 7.
208. The contacts 1925–1927 are very briefly recounted by Gaius Glenn Atkins and Frederick L. Fagley, *History of American Congregationalism* (Boston: Pilgrim Press, 1942), p. 356.

209. *Excluded,* op. cit. n. 165, pp. i, 2ff. Cummins endeavors to refute Clinton Lee Scott's more pro-Christian interpretation of the attempts in *A History,* pp. 43–45; cf. Cummins, *Parish Practice in the Universalist Churches* (Boston: Murray Press, 1946) and *Universalist Church of America,* op. cit. n. 113. Some of the clerical and much of the lay support for entry into the Council stemmed from a concern for Christian identity.

210. Above, at n. 163, ch. 2.

211. Above, at n. 209, this chapter. On the inherent problem in the context of the problematic of world religion, see Zwi Werblowsky, "Universal Religion and Universalist Religion," *International Association for Religious Freedom Information Service,* No. 67/68 (Spring 1870), pp. 58–71.

212. James Minton Pullman, "Exposition of Universalism," *The Winchester Centennial 1803–1903: Historical Sketch* (Boston: Universalist Publishing House, 1903). He continues, "The Universalist faith is absolute belief in an adequate God who is able to conduct his universe to the goal of his desires without inflicting an eternal catastrophe upon any of his creatures."

213. Ibid., p. 149. He goes on: "For this ["the moral product"] the fleeting generations come and go; and the stream of human life and the storm of human action have their chief significance in the fact that in the roaring loom of time some human character is being woven." Earlier at the Columbus Congress (1893), Pullman in "Universalism and the World's Faith," *loc. cit.,* pp. 341–348, has declared with reference to an older eschatology, that "there are no 'lost things' in sight" and that "Man's progress is interminable." Printed also by Shinn in *Good Tidings,* op. cit. n. 13, pp. 149–156.

214. *1770–1920,* op. cit. n. 199, p. 70. The paper was not printed, nor does it appear in Alan Seaburg's complete calendared bibliography, "The Writings of Dean Skinner." *Journal of the Universalist Historical Society, V* (1964–65), pp. 65–77 with curriculum vitae, p. 65.

215. *Unity, LXXXIII* (July 31, 1919), p. 259.

216. Preached before the Boston Association of Universalists in Waltham, MA, May 7, 1890, and printed in *The Christian Leader, LX* (May 22, 1890), p. 2 in 6 columns with pictures and sketch. Grandfather Skinner also published an appreciative essay on John Wesley, in whom he saw a prototype of John Murray's break from the New England religious establishment, *UQGR, I* (1894), pp. 486–500.

217. Published (posthumously) in *Worship and a Well Ordered Life,* ed. by Alfred S. Cole (Boston: Universalist Historical Society and Meeting House Press, 1955), pp. 1–33. James D. Hunt deals genetically and systematically with Skinner's idea of the Church in "The Liberal Theology of Clarence R.

Skinner," *Journal of the Universalist Historical Society, VII* (1967–68), pp. 110–115.

218. Cf. Jerry V. Caswell, "A New Civilization," *Journal of the Universalist Historical Society, VII* (1967–1968), pp. 70–96.
219. *Theologically Speaking,* first issue (leaflet series), c. 1945, p. 12.
220. *Ibid.,* pp. 9f.

Conclusion

1. Above, at n. 16, ch. 2.
2. Appleton, quoted above, at n. 4, Introduction.
3. John Murray, *The Life of Rev. John Murray,* centennial ed. (Boston: Munroe and Francis, 1870), p. 190.

INDEX

John 12:47, 3
Acts 3:21, 106
Acts 10:34, 96
Rom. 5:6, 3
I Cor. 15:22, 3
Eph. 5:25, 15
Col. 1:20, 3
I Tim. 1:17, 33
I Tim. 2:4, 3
I Tim. 3:15, 93
II Pet. 3:8, 8
Jude 3:6, 3
Rev. 14:6, 85
Rev. 22:13, 8
Seaburg, Alan, 87, 102, 114
Seitz, Don C., 99
Selleck, Willard C., 68, 70
Shakespeare, 70
Shinn, Quillen Hamilton, 32, 42, 52,
    54-55, 67, 82, 100
    theology, 35-37
Shutter, Marion D., 112
Siegvolck, Paul. *See* Georg Klein-Nikolai
Skinner, Charles Augustus, 76
Skinner, Charles Montgomery, 76
Skinner, Clarence Russell, 24, 31, 49-50,
    63, 76-77, 115
Skinner, George W., 10-11, 18
Sophia, 86
Soule, Caroline A., 41
Spear, Charles, 53, 54, 108
Spear, John Murray, 53-54
Spencer, Herbert, 10
Stone, E. M., 103
Stonehouse, Sir James, 3, 85
Sutton, Katherine A., 100
Sweetser, Edwin C., 63, 69-70
Tarbell, Ida M., 105
Taylor, John, 89
Tennant, Gilbert, 87

Thayer, Thomas Baldwin, 5, 46, 59, 92-93
Thomas, Abel C., 46, 100
Thoreau, Henry D., 108
Thun, Nils, 86
Tolstoy, Leo, 57
Tomlinson, Vincent E., 99, 113
Turner, Edward, 91
Tuveson, Ernest Lee, 95
Tuttle, J. H., 23
Upham, Thomas Cogswell, 108
Vickery, Charles, 111
Victor Emmanuel, 90
Vidler, William, x
Vinton, Jennie, 102
Wallace, Robert, 92
Ware, Henry, Sr., 81
Warne, Colston E., 104
Warner, Charles Dudley, 107
Washburn, Israel, 6, 18-23, 81
Washington, George, 21
Wayne, Anthony, 102
Weaver, George Sumner, 109
Werblowsky, Zwi, 114
Wesley, John, 87, 89, 93, 114
West, Mrs. George, 104
Whitfield, George, 87
Whittemore, Thomas, xii, 9-10, 13, 19, 53
Wilbur, Earl Morse, 8
Williams, John E., 99
Willis, Gwendolyn, 101
Willis, John Henry, 101
Wilson, Walter, 86
Winchester, Elhanan, x, 3-5, 7, 10, 18,
    25, 45, 65, 80, 81, 85
Wolley, Robert S., 102
Wood, Jacob, 25
Woodman, Richard M., 110
Wright, C. Conrad, 89, 91
Wright, Fanny, 34
Young, Owen D., 50-51

ACKNOWLEDGMENTS

For help in the preparation and completion of this Essay, I wish to thank Theodore Webb, President of the Universalist Historical Society; James D. Hunt, editor of the *Journal* of the Society; David A. Johnson, Alan Seaburg, Carl Seaburg, and Mrs. Jeanne Harrison Nieuwejaar, gracious and helpful librarian of the Universalist Historical Library (henceforth UHL) at Tufts University; my Harvard colleague C. Conrad Wright, and Harvard Divinity School students, Robert Shaw ('72) and especially John Buehrens ('72).

The reader's attention should be called to the following: Alan L. Seaburg, "Recent Scholarship in American Universalism: A Bibliographical Essay," pp. 513–523 in the Dec. 1972 issue of *Church History;* also the forthcoming two volume history of American Universalism by Russell Miller.

GHW
1971